HORSE SENSE:

A Lifetime Love Story

By

Doug Heser
& Cheryl J. Heser

DEDICATION:

To George and Lucille Canfield,
who taught me most of what I know
about horses and their handling and uses.
They would have loved this book.

When we were first going together, Cherie and I went to an old-fashioned barn dance at Canfields' ranch. George met her, asked her to dance, and told her he would dance at our wedding. Sure enough, he did! They were a wonderful part of our lives until George died. After that, Lucille had us out to the ranch and came to visit us at Harlowton before she passed away.

Doug Heser

George and Lucille in the Richey, Montana, parade, fall of 1978.

George drove a team with this wagon for the movie "The Hooker Bunch," filmed in Red Lodge. He doubled for Dub Taylor. When the movie was completed, George acquired the Dr. Hooker wagon, and as far as I know, it is still at their place. George got a kick out of doing that.

Doug and Pardner, Heser home place northeast of Vida, 1975

How wonderful to have
The West in your soul.
To have blue skies over your head
And brown earth and rich grass
Under your feet.
To live a life so close to the earth
And its creatures that you know
That the sunrise every morning
Is the smile of the Creator.

C. J. Heser

TABLE OF CONTENTS

FORWARD:

All of my teen and adult life has involved horses. I love them, and as I increased in knowledge of dealing with horses, I came to believe that they love me – or at least respect me, which is crucial to the relationship. Now I get to share some of that love, respect, and know-how, and I hope you enjoy it.

Right now, I have four horses in my string. From oldest to youngest are Bandit, an average-size pinto good for some regular horse work because of his age but also a good kids' horse; Comet, a slim black gelding great for heeling calves and regular cow work, 20 years old and capable but good at saving himself; Ace, an average-sized bay horse with an excellent disposition, a good traveling all-around horse; and Tucker, a big brown gelding who is the best-built horse I've ever owned, originally trained by our son Josh and a very capable horse who can really run and work but you have to get it out of him – he will shirk!

From the time that I first met Cheryl (Cherie, to me), I have been telling her stories about horses, and of course, she has lived many of those stories with me. She claims she fell in love with me when I was riding Shane, a horse you will get to know well in these pages. We have now been married for 50 years, so maybe it's time to tell Shane's story along with many others.

This journey has a sad side. My dad was a master storyteller with a real sense of history and a delightful sense of humor. He always told stories. It was an adventure to go for a Sunday ride with him in northern McCone County, Montana, where I grew up because he could identify every homestead place and tell us stories about the people who lived there, what happened to them, and who owned the place now.

Sadly, Dad died too young, and none of those stories were recorded or written down. I remember some, but of course, the bulk of that wisdom and history is gone with him. Last year when I turned 75, Cherie insisted that my stories should not go the way of my dad's. With that idea in mind, the concept of this book emerged, and I began retelling the stories that we have enjoyed together through the years.

The stories take place in various places all over eastern and central Montana. For the last 35 years, my home country has been central and northern Rosebud County, in the southeast part of Montana east of Billings and west of the North Dakota border. We currently live north of Forsyth but spent a number of years living in the tiny burg of Rosebud, 10 miles east of Forsyth.

A major part of my life since 1995 has been spent at a ranch camp north of Forsyth on Little Porcupine Creek Road called the Radeen Place as well as at Dog Creek, 26 miles to the east. Both of them are part of the Montgomery Ranch. In between are the Trail Creek and Ryan's Fork pastures, each about 29 sections, where much of my riding will be set. I always enjoy thinking of all the parts of Montana where I have left "pony tracks" and seen my share of beauty from the back of one member of my favorite species of animal.

Doug Heser,
May 2024

CHAPTER 1

HORSES IN GENERAL

Horses are fascinating animals, one of the rare animals which has been valued since ancient times for all possible uses of an animal. They are, of course, used as recreational animals, show animals, and work animals and for racing, polo, and other sports. Horses are also increasingly valued for use in therapy for PTSD and psychological conditions and for troubled teens and youngsters with handicaps.

We usually think of horses for riding use, but in some cultures, their meat is a main part of the diet, and in ancient times their milk was consumed regularly. In central Asia today, fermented mare's milk is used for making alcoholic beverages. Personally, I'll eat beef steak and drink my corn-based bourbon! Horse uses vary, of course, but as a breeding animal, they produce offspring for sale, made even more valuable by training.

From a rich person's investment to a poor person's work companion, horses move about in all parts of our society other than inner cities, although even there you might see a mounted policeman or a rodeo, even in Madison Square Garden! However, something about a horse goes beyond these practical uses and considerations. What makes people, from kids to old cowboys, love horses? For one thing, they make good companions. I had one horse I called Pardner, and the way he worked with me, he was as good a pardner as I will ever have – and I've worked with some very fine men and women.

Second, a horse's eyes are a compelling reason to love them. Because they are prey rather than predator, their eyes are set on the sides of the head and can often be soft and very beautiful. Horses look at you as though they understand, and often I think they do. Many horses are truly "gentle giants," large and powerful but non-threatening. Some are exceptions, but they are fewer, and most but not all can be gentled through training.

Third, personality makes horses loveable. I will be telling many stories about horse laggards, high work-ethic chargers, determined travelers, and so on. At times their love of people and of other horses goes beyond, as I will share with the tale of my lanky gelding Shane and the filly foal he adopted and then missed for days when she was sold and gone.

Finally, horses provide a way for a person to go above and beyond what he is capable of when he is afoot, a way to get a long ways over country that a vehicle cannot travel, and a way to get jobs done efficiently, such as rescuing or treating livestock. In addition, horses have always provided a way for me to escape for a while, get away from problems, enjoy the beauty of the natural world, and restore my resolution to go on with all of life. Sitting atop a horse, I watched a baby antelope being born and observed a mother badger waddling down a game trail followed by three baby badgers. How many people get to see something like that?

"Horse Sense" is a product of all of these things, based on my love of horses and my desire to share some good stories with those who love horses, too. And, perhaps, those who will come to love horses a little more just because I shared some stories.

CHAPTER 2

A LITTLE KNOW-HOW ABOUT HORSES

A good traveling horse is an enjoyable way to get across country, gather and work with cattle, and sometimes run other horses. Horses don't require a lot of maintenance, just hay when needed, oats, grazing, and good water. Grazing can be whatever Mother Nature provides. Horses don't need a lot of high protein and don't need much in the way of minerals. In some areas with different soil compositions, they will eat more salt. Another maintenance is to trim their feet once in a while. Horses can work at just about any temperature and have a good tolerance for cold. When it gets to be 100 degrees, they can be used but you have to be careful because most horses will play out quicker in that kind of heat.

The average life expectancy varies in horses just as in all animals, but in general, a good horse will be sound until he is 20 years old. Some go on being healthy and useful after that, but some cripple up with leg and feet troubles before that. Those problems with legs and feet are usually their biggest problem. Trimming hooves is essential to help with that problem.

One thing I learned in dealing with maintenance on a lot of horses was the correct way to trim hooves. Horsemen must keep their horses' feet trimmed to prevent cracking and breaking off, which can cause them to be sore and/or lame. Horses with thick-walled feet can have feet grow out too long, and it's just like a person wearing a boot two or three sizes too big. Feet can also grow out too long from foundering on too much grain or areas with a lack of selenium in the soil where horses founder on green grass.

I use nippers for trimming and then a horse rasp to smooth the edges. Beyond proper trimming, a lot of foot problems can be corrected by proper shoeing. Especially in rocky country, horses should be shod. Traction for special uses like rodeoing depends on good shoeing, also. I can add ere that some horses are cooperative and easy to trim and shoe and other horses will make you really work for success! Bandit knocked out my front tooth and another time damaged my face with a lead rope. Our old, gentle part-time kids' horse? Yep, that's the one!

Of course, other parts of horse bodies can be vulnerable. I had one horse with a real problem with his spine and lower back after he twisted coming down a steep hill. A horse chiropractor really helped. Mouths are also a concern. Older horses can develop teeth problems, and a good veterinary can float the teeth, which helps unless they begin losing teeth as well. In Montana, we deal with rattlesnakes, and a snake bite in the mouth can actually cause a horse's head to swell up and can prevent eating and drinking.

A crucial part of buying, training, and dealing with horses is learning horse conformation. What am I looking for? First, proper muscling, a long hip, a round butt, a short back but a long underline, and legs that are up under the horse and come down close together. Muscling over the loin indicates a strong back. The whole back should be muscled but not overly muscled. A well-conformed horse will have a prominent wither above the shoulder blades. Front legs and back legs should "V" from the chest to the knees and from the hip down to the hocks.

I look for short cannon bones in the front legs from the knee down to the pastern, which flexes above the foot. Pasterns should be fairly long with a good slope for a smooth ride. Hooves should be steep enough so that the hairline is off the ground. Black hooves aren't as hard in the summer and aren't as prone to crack as white hooves. A horse's neck should be long and trim, about the same length as the top of the back. The head should be consistent with the rest of the body and fairly trim, not Roman-nosed and pig-eyed, traits which usually indicate that the horse is a bucker.

I have always taken special note of horse dispositions. Some are very nervous; some are calm and usually reliable. Some are lazy;

some really want to work. Some get bored and mischievous, including those who stay coltish all their lives. The coltish ones will play with things like flopping around sacks and can get into trouble, figuring out how to open gates, often looking for an excuse to spook at something. How does a good rider deal with these things? When riding, we don't let them spook, and often it works to show them what they're spooking at. We stay alert to what they're looking at and what they're thinking, and we stay on top of anything the horse chooses to do.

With a haphazard horse, what gets done is up to the rider. With a willing horse, he'll contribute a lot. I think 70% horse and 30% rider is ideal. Keeping good footing and an attentive eye is up to the horse. Situations like balancing a horse is the rider's responsibility, as well as maintaining the right position going downhill, going uphill, or crossing a coulee. Leg position helps a horse turn and stop. Many trainers put most of the emphasis on reining, which is important, but leg position and pressure are even more important. Excellent riders can demonstrate controlling a horse with no reins at all.

A smart owner/rider soon identifies the attitude of the horse under him. The reliable ones will pick things up fast and be willing to do whatever's at hand. The more they are used, the better they get. The lazy ones don't care to travel and don't care if they get the job done. So, what does a person do? Ride, keep pedaling, keep spurring them along. Most of all, don't let little habits grow into big habits. Things like spooking, bucking, getting distracted, and not paying attention need to be dealt with at the time and corrected. Otherwise, riders might find themselves losing the cattle or even sitting on the ground dealing with cactus spines. In our country, we always say cactus makes good riders!

We've all heard plenty about "horse whisperers." I'm probably not in that category, but I do believe in the method of horsemanship like that used by Ray Hunt. Basically, it's a gentle method based on being in tune with the horse and having the horse in tune with you. As I worked with horses, I developed a sixth sense about the horse and what he was going to do as well as how he was responding to what I wanted him to do.

On the ground during training, I look for signs like a horse licking his lips, which shows he is relaxing. I notice when he is cocking his ears forward or paying attention by cocking an ear back toward me and bending his head toward me. When I am on the ground, I really want that eye contact. As my son Clint has even noted in a church sermon, submission is the beginning of a good relationship with the rider. I work a young horse systematically, demanding that he move when I want him to move and stop when I want him to stop. I want him to face me, and sometimes that takes a while for a young horse to learn. However, once he reaches that stage, which always gets acknowledged with some nose or cheek petting, he can be trained to regularly come to me, lead well, and pay attention to everything else he has to learn.

When I'm riding a horse, green or experienced, what am I looking for? First, like on the ground, I watch their ears. The ears should be attentive, moving back and forth, both pointed forward when they're looking at something strange or if they are confident about what they're doing. A colt will work the ears more, trying to figure things out. If the ears are flat against their head, they're mad. That's a good time to feel if the horse is tensing up, he's scared, or about to buck. Tenseness will communicate itself through the rider's legs and knees. The best thing to do is to walk the horse in tight circles or do roll-backs, which is a move where the horse spins on his hind feet. When I feel them relax a bit, then I get them to walk away and leave them alone.

In addition to observing the ears, a good rider is aware of the horse's nose, a sign that he is not only looking ahead but also keeping an eye on the ground. If the nose is flat, held straight out, the horse can't see the ground as well. I've even seen professional barrel racers with the problem of a horse holding its nose straight out and, as a result, turning poorly or knocking over barrels. Also, if the nose is out, often the horse is not collected to pivot or stop. Again, this reminds us of the importance of the horse's partnership in what happens.

What else is important? The horse should be in the right lead, which means he's using the right or left front foot first depending on the direction he's going. Lead changes are essential in smooth turning, as can be observed watching correct pole bending or barrel racing. I have to mention that our daughter Anne won Horsemanship I in 4-H on a pony because several times she corrected the pony's lead and the judge was impressed.

Above all, a good rider will be aware of what the horse is going to do, although we all get surprised once in a while! Because ranch horse owners deal regularly with cattle, we want a horse with cow sense, literally a sense for observing cattle and figuring out what they are going to do and what it will take to deal with them. Some horses just naturally have cow sense and some don't; but with both kinds of horses, the more cattle they are around, the better they get. Some lines of quarter horses have a natural instinct for moving cattle, most noticeable in cutting horses, which are horses specially trained and used for cutting out cattle (which means separating them from other cattle) both in competition and in ranch use.

Crossbred horses can develop cow sense. My big old gelding Shane, who was a Percheron workhorse/thoroughbred cross, had more cow sense, especially in a corral, than most quarter horses I have ridden. Finally, if you are dealing with huge pastures like the 29-section Trail Creek pasture I gather often, it's fun to have a horse that can get on a long trot and go forever. My first horse, Chief, had a long trot and could cover eight miles in less than an hour. I've enjoyed that quality in a horse ever since.

Of course, as a rider, a person needs to be aware of the individual horse he's using. But awareness must also include other horses and other riders and what they are doing. A good horse will be aware as well but also with maturity will not be distracted by other horses unless they are doing something really noticeable like bucking. An owner of more than one horse also needs to be knowledgeable about horses in groups.

Horses are social animals who prefer to be with other horses, but when they are in a group, they definitely have a pecking order. We've had older horses who could be plenty mean when keeping their dominance over the group – and especially over the feed! A really dominant, antagonistic horse can cause problems for other horses, even driving them into barbed wire fences. Sometimes, horses need to be isolated to deal with the problems they are causing. As much as I like my big gelding Tucker, I isolate him during morning feeding so that all the horses get fed equally.

CHAPTER 3

CHIEF

I grew up on a farm in northeastern Montana as the oldest of three brothers with a younger sister. We boys were all interested in horses and riding and got started using an old workhorse and then a pony. But Chief was our first real horse. After a rodeo in Wolf Point, one of Rodeo Producer Marvin Brookman's studs got out and got with the local eye doctor's pen of thoroughbred brood mares. The next spring, there was a little homely, Roman-nosed paint stud colt, and the doctor was not happy at all. A Roman nose, for your information, is a nose that curves around instead of coming straight down the way you would expect in a horse.

Gene Martin, a local saddle-maker, bought the colt, broke him to ride, and named him Chief. Our dad bought him for us kids. He was a young horse but perfect for kids to learn on. He had a good mouth, reined well, could travel, and didn't have any buck in him. I learned to ride Chief mostly by trial and error.

Chief had some tricks. A neighbor borrowed him one time, brought him back, and told us he was limping. My brother went back and rode with the neighbor, and right away Chief wasn't limping anymore. Every now and then Chief would paw into a wire gate. When we came out in the morning, he would be standing with a foot over the bottom wire waiting for us to get it out for him. We rode Chief for fun, but we also used him to help our uncle and the neighbors with cattle. That was farming country with a lot of farmers who ran some cows but weren't horsemen and depended on the horsemen around to help out when cattle needed moving or branding. We helped neighbors for a lot of years. Chief didn't have a lot of cow sense, but neither did we.

I liked horseback riding right off. For one thing, it didn't involve sitting on a back-breaking tractor and eating a lot of dust! Ever since that time, I have far preferred ranching to farming, mostly because of horses. Horseback riding offered freedom and the enjoyment of developing new skills. We teenagers spent most of our time at a trot but galloped when it was needed. We had Chief for a number of years. I rode him from the time I was a sophomore in high school until after I returned from the Army at age 21. He developed a cracked bone and limped on his front foot. A neighbor bought him and rested him a year, and he was fine. By then we had moved on to other horses.

CHAPTER 4

EARLY EXPERIENCES BREAKING HORSES;

MEET THE CANFIELDS!

I started breaking horses when I was a junior in high school. This is a good time to define the term "breaking." Despite the old-west picture of riding a bronc into the dust -- literally breaking his spirit -- breaking in the sense I use it is far different, although some exciting riding might be part of the picture. A good horseman starts with halter breaking, something which, when done right, teaches the horse not only how to be caught and to lead but also how to respect and respond to his trainer. Then comes bridling and saddling, followed by stepping on the horse in a corral and quietly teaching him to carry a rider. After that, a trainer graduates to teach reining and advanced use.

We brothers broke four or five horses for a neighbor named Earl Good. Starting with barely halter-broken horses, we didn't do a lot of ground work but just saddled them up and started riding them. They were pretty cold-blooded and gentle and didn't offer to buck, which was a good thing, because we weren't exactly ready for Charlie Russell's "Bronc to Breakfast"! Then we broke two appaloosas for Earl's brother George. We worked on plow reining first, which is done two-handed, and then gradually neck reining. We worked on getting them to stop and roping with them. We used spurs with some of them, especially if they were slow and lazy. At that point, we didn't know anything about rollbacks and pivots and side-passing and all of the other skills I would learn later.

When I really started learning about all of the techniques for dealing with horses, it was with George Canfield. George had a place on the Redwater River near Richey, Montana, where he raised cattle, a rodeo string, and brood mares. George would work with colts, first getting them to face up to him. He'd get them hobble broke, which means standing still with leather hobbles around their feet. That's needed knowledge if a horse needs to be kept near until the rider uses him again. George would sack the colts out, flopping a saddle blanket around on them. Then he'd saddle them and let them stand for a brief bit of time. After they relaxed about it, he'd turn them loose and let them pack the saddle for a while.

The next day George would hang a snaffle bit in the horse's mouth, tie the bridle reins to the cinch, and get the horses to flexing. Then he'd ground drive them around in a circle. For your information, a snaffle bit is the most common type of bit used while riding horses. It consists of a bit mouthpiece with a ring on each side and acts with direct pressure. George would run a rein from each side of the snaffle bit through the stirrup leathers to the back of the horse. That got them bridle-wise. Then he would put the bridle on and start riding them. He would ride them around in the corral a lot, getting them to turn and travel out free. Then he would ride them outside and again get them to travel free. In the spring we would be able to use the young horses for gathering cattle, moving cattle, branding, etc.

From 1966 until I went into the Army in August of 1967, I worked for George and his wife Lucille on their spread. Lucille was the daughter of a teamster, and she could drive horses pulling a wagon to town when she was eight years old. George and Lucille were as knowledgeable about horse conformation as anyone I ever worked with. They also were as knowledgeable about handling livestock as anyone.

Life on the Canfield Ranch was never dull! George and I cut studs for neighbor rancher Dale Waters, 34 in one day. They were young Appaloosas from two to four years old. George was excellent at fore-footing a horse, roping the front feet, and tying three legs together. Then we would pull the top hind leg up high so that the horse could be castrated. I'm sure to a non-horse person, this sounds cruel. But it's actually a quick process and usually heals quickly and easily. Castrated horses called geldings are much more useful for ranch horses, and it's a rare stud that works well with other horses. I worked with George, my brother Ike, and two other cowboys to get that job done. That was a big day!

George led an adventurous life and had to have a little excitement along with the work and obligations. He just loved to tell stories about the times that the excitement took over, and taking a break or eating lunch with him at a branding was always a colorful time.

One time George and two neighbors were trucking some horses, and they looked out the side windows and the horses were running along beside them. They stopped and caught the horses and reloaded them, but the end gate had fallen off and they couldn't get it held back on. They were near an old country school and "borrowed" the flagpole to tie in the end gate. Of course, the pole stuck way up above the truck. They went on down the road telling stories and discovered in the rearview mirror that they were dragging a bunch of wires. Those were the old fence-line telephone wires that were run up over the road at crossroads, and the flagpole had hooked the wires, broken them off, and pulled them along behind the truck. Of course, the men ended up with some fixing and explaining to do, but George would tell the story, slap the table, and laugh so hard.

George ran Canfield Rodeo, which supplied bulls, steers, and bucking horses to amateur rodeos all around eastern and central Montana. Dealing with bucking horses took some skill because the horses knew what was happening and would just as soon stay on Redwater River where the grass was good. George knew how to handle them, getting them corralled and loaded. Of course, he and the crew were constantly dealing with single-axle semis, driving on muddy roads, and loading cattle onto the trucks through the chutes. It was always a challenge and always exciting.

We had three truck wrecks in one year, one empty and two with bucking horses loaded on. One driver spent a little too much time at the beer garden and tipped the truck over on the way home. The horses kicked the top out of the truck and unloaded themselves. They were on the highway, and George had to find a corral where they could gather them and reload them on a different truck. The third wreck was the funniest one, when George was driving a truck east of Vida, ran into rain, and the trailer slid into the ditch and tipped the whole thing over. George climbed out, sat on the hood, and said, "My insurance man isn't going to like to hear about this!" He kept the horses at a neighbor's place for part of the summer and then trailed them home.

George loved to break teams to drive, and I enjoyed it, too. He had a pair of smaller Welsh/Arabian crosses, and we broke them to drive that winter. He would get them sacked out and harnessed and teach them to stay together while he ground-drove them. When they handled fairly decently, he would hook them up to a sleigh with a running W, a rope from the seat to one front leg, then through a ring, then to another front leg of both horses. If they got to running too hard, he could pull on the rope, and it takes their front feet away from them and puts them down to their knees. After they were pretty dependable, he would drive them with lines and spend a lot of time just driving them.

That sleigh has a special place in my wife's memory. We were newly married, and that winter Canfields invited us to their place for supper and told us they had a surprise for us. They harnessed up a team to the sleigh and bundled us all in with blankets. Then we took off for a beautiful ride with the moon and stars shining and the snow glinting off the trees and hillsides. George took the sleigh all around the hills and along the frozen river, with genuine sleighbells jingling and the sounds of the horses' hooves and deep breathing. Cherie was sure she was dreaming!

Lucille grew up driving teams from an early age for her dad and was very capable. She also was in on buying and selling a lot of horses. There was a horse cannery in North Platte, Nebraska, where they would take loads of canner horses. When George and Lucille were first married, she spent a lot of time with horses. She handled the business end of Canfield Rodeo along with teaching math at the Richey School. They always had a brood mare band, and Lucille raised horses even after George died. She gave us a pair of albino horses. They were fascinating – blue eyes and white almost pink noses.

George taught me to break horses, to handle livestock including roping steers, sorting pairs, cutting out dries, etc. I learned most of what I know about horses, riding, and livestock handling from George. He was not patient about it, but he sure taught me a lot and expected me to measure up. One time he and his son Tiny were feeding little square bales. George was riding. Tiny fished a raccoon out of a stack. George was trying to get him chased back to the pickup so that Tiny could shoot him, and the coon started to climb the horse's front leg. George got bucked off and nursed some pretty good bruises. That horse was Rawhide, a good-using paint quarter horse, but you didn't want to get into a wreck with him.

One year at branding time, a neighbor rancher named Bob Delp was riding Rawhide and was using George's old saddle, which had seen way too many miles. Bob roped a calf and dragged him just about to the fire when the front D-rings of the saddle broke. The saddle tipped back, Bob got thrown off, and the horse ran through the branding and made two circles, bucking and kicking at the saddle until all that was left was the throat latch and brow band on the bridle, and the saddle was lying out in the middle of the arena.

Needless to say, all branding activity stopped for the show. I was right behind Bob, waiting to drag a calf in, and I looked up, and there was Bob on the ground and the horse bucking right through the fire. After the excitement was over and everyone was okay,

George put a different bridle and saddle on Rawhide. I rode him for the rest of the branding, but I was definitely careful with him!

Trucking horses was always a challenge. One time George took a load of horses to a sale in Ohio. Coming back through Chicago, they got lost and had to get advice from a state trooper to get off the highway, and headed back to Rapid City, South Dakota. He preferred to put a truck through the backroads, even when it was muddy or dicey, and city driving wasn't for him.

CHAPTER 5

SHANE

Shane was a colt out of Canfields' thoroughbred stud and a Percheron cross mare named Blue Goose, who bucked at the National Finals. I trained him as a young horse and enjoyed every day of working with him. My wife always said she fell in love with me when I was riding Shane, both of us tall, dark, and handsome (at least Shane was!). I have credited Shane for strengthening our early marriage. My former fiancée owned Shane at that time, and she called and demanded him back unless I paid for him. At a time when we had little to no money, my wife unhesitatingly told me she would send the check and Shane would be mine. I loved her even more for that decision, and we made it financially.

As an adult horse, Shane was 16 hands, big and lazy – one of those horses that take good care of themselves. But he was probably as good a horse as I ever rode for sorting pairs out of a bunch and working in a corral. His strong point was that he saw the cow you were after at the same time you did. That quality is called "cow sense" or being "cow-y," and it is something I have always valued in a good horse. Some like Shane have it naturally and some develop it over time to some degree or another.

For a big horse, Shane could turn on a dime. He very seldom got out-ducked by a cow trying to get past him and back in the bunch. I broke him and used him and eventually owned him. He was part of my life for the rest of his. I used him for branding and cattle work of all kinds. My wife used to laugh because I would come in the house cussing Shane for being lazy and making me work for everything I got out of him. And the next day I would use him in the corral and come in the house telling her that was the best horse I'd ever had. I never really had a wreck with him and could depend on him to be pretty sensible.

The most fun stories of Shane involve our daughter Anne when she was about 11 years old. She was entered in Showmanship for 4-H, and she had outgrown her pony and was using Shane. He would do anything for her even if he was anything but a show horse. She won Junior Showmanship and ended up in the Round Robin, where the kids had to show a horse, a steer, a sheep, and a pig. Shane looked around and discovered he was the only horse and was stuck in with those other animals, and you could actually see the disdain on his face. From that point on, he wouldn't do anything for anyone. Anne worked and worked to get him to set up and lead and do things for the judge, and he just wouldn't. Her friend Clay Espy was there with his steer and was also a competent horseman, and he couldn't get him to do anything either.

Anne was also entered in Horsemanship II, and Shane had on my big, heavy saddle, which I helped her with. The judge surprised the kids by asking them to unsaddle and resaddle their horses. Anne's eyes got saucer-sized, but she managed to undo the cinches and pull that big saddle and blanket off Shane. Then she worked and worked and rolled the cinch and right stirrup up onto the saddle, pulled it up to her knees, and then managed to heave the saddle back onto his back, a little crooked but up there. Shane just patiently waited until the whole thing was finished. She did well in the class and loved Shane for the rest of his life.

Shane was with us everywhere we lived, from the farm near Vida to a ranch south of Harlowton and then our little place west of Harlowton, to a ranch at Judith Gap, then a ranch on the Powder River out of Broadus, then to Rosebud and finally to our current place north of Forsyth. He adapted easily everywhere he lived and got to know the country and the cattle right along with me. When we lived in the small town of Rosebud, we had to pasture the horses with an elderly former nurse named Jean Melle. She loved the horses, kept them fed in the winter, and once in a while rode one of them. Jean thought a lot of Shane, but she kept her riding to the shorter horses like Eagle, for good reason.

20

Because the horses were pastured out but used by me for work and by the kids for helping me and for 4-H, they had to be loaded and transported a lot. I had a one-ton Chevy truck with a heavy homemade end gate, and although it wasn't as easy to use as a horse trailer, it sure worked for getting the horses where we needed them. Shane always loaded right up, whether it was into that truck or into a horse trailer. Maybe his easy loading was partly due to all the places he had been moved, but like many horses, he had the disposition to just get busy and get into the trailer. It was a sad day when he took his last trailer ride to the plant where his life ended mercifully.

Doug on Shane, heeling at a branding, late April 1985

A HORSE CALLED SHANE

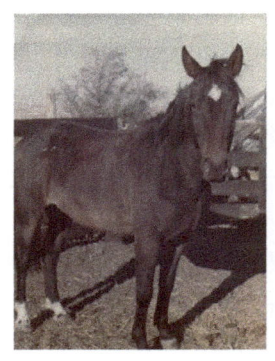

Let me tell you about a horse called Shane,
Good all-around gelding, old Western style.
He'd carry a man through good and bad times
And over many a Montana mile.

Sired by a proud, tall thoroughbred stud
And a workhorse rodeo mare, Blue Goose,
He stood well over sixteen hands tall
And could go when he wanted to turn it loose.

A lanky brown horse with shades of black,
White star and dark, intelligent eyes,
He trained so easy and had cow sense,
And from age two was part of our lives,

He'd think ahead of a man with a rope
And in a corral could turn on a dime;
His gait was rough; he could cover ground,
But he'd carry a kid and take his time.

One day an old Hereford made him mad:
When the rope caught fast, Shane gave no slack
But hit the end with all of his might
And tossed that cow right onto her back!

Now Shane just loved both horses and folks
And especially liked the county fair.
He could socialize to his heart's delight
And pig out on hay and pellets there.

For showmanship with his little cowgirl,
He showed such pride in his stance and eyes.
He did everything that she asked and more,
And helped her to win the champion prize.

But he loved the hills best, a man on his back,
Cattle to chase and a job to do,
For deep inside of that lanky frame
Beat the heart of a cowhorse, tried and true.

After twenty-five years of memories,
Old Shane, it hurts to have to part,
For it's easy to find a horse that's good,
But it's special to know a horse with heart.

--C.J. Heser

22

CHAPTER 6

IKE

Ike was a horse I broke for Bob Thomas, a rancher on Sand Creek south of Wolf Point. Ike was a big, homely, rat-tail Appaloosa with a Roman nose. I commented earlier that a Roman nose sometimes indicates a bucker, but Ike, like Chief, was an exception to that rule. He wore a #2 shoe as a three-year-old, something that shows you how big his hooves were. He stood 16 hands high, which puts him among the taller horses. Ike was a good son-of-a-gun. He was a horse who could trot all day and had outstanding endurance. I liked to use him to heel calves at branding. He didn't have a lot of cow sense, but he was sure willing.

Where I really learned to love Ike was when it was wet and we were crossing a badland coulee and started up the other side. His front feet slipped out from under him, and he fell to his knees and slid backward. He never panicked, never reacted, just got to the bottom. He stood up, and we found another way to get out of the coulee. From that point on, I knew he was a horse I could trust and depend on.

About six months after I was gone working elsewhere and had returned Ike, the owner called me to help gather cattle. He hauled me out to the far end of the pasture. I stepped on Ike, and it was like we had never had a break. I sure enjoyed the day on him.

One time the next spring, I was working for a rancher named Bud Long for branding. I rode Ike again. He humped up a little but then settled right down. Bud, who was a character, said, "Too bad he doesn't have something better for you to ride than him." I just nodded and didn't comment because homely or not, Ike was a great mount. Bob sold Ike to his son-in-law who took him to the mountains and used him as a hunting horse. He sure traveled those mountain trails, and his endurance really paid off.

Ike was an honest ranch horse. That means a horse who doesn't fudge and does whatever the rider wants him to do. I have ridden horses who were lazy, wanted to buck, never saw a cow, and always wanted to head back home instead of finishing the job. Often, they were constantly looking for another horse. I have always valued honest horses like Ike, and of course, I look for that trait when I buy a horse, although sometimes it is hard to tell until a person has put some miles on one.

CHAPTER 7

HORSES AT WARNER JOHNSON'S RANCH

During the winters of 70-71 and 71-72, I worked for Warner Johnson, a rancher out of Brockway, Montana. The first winter I broke roughly 40 horses, two-year-olds to four-year-olds, some of them pretty bronchy. It was a cold, snowy winter, and I had to ride them in a 40X80 shed. Warner threw the junk up against the walls and set up some portable panels. On nice days, I would take as many as I could outside for some time traveling. The second year was a little easier winter and I could ride outside more. Most of the horses turned out really well.

During that first year, Warner had a green four-year-old stud. I had him going in the corrals and outside. I would take that stud and go up a lane to the east and gather the mares. One day the lane was solidly drifted. I made the stud wade through as much snow as I could and went clear around the outside hoping to get some hard miles on him before I ran into the mares. As luck would have it, they were in the middle of the pasture.

When the stud got wind of them, he just took off. I got behind them the best I could and hollered to get them running. We headed uphill, and the stud got high-centered in the drifts. He just stopped. I got off, and he floundered through the snowbank. I got back on, and luckily the mares headed for home and we trotted along behind them. That experience really made a good horse out of him. He was excellent at moving horses after that.

I rode a lot of the horses for calving time, especially the older ones. I was riding a mare who was on the bronchy side. There was a cow in a reservoir, and I roped her and couldn't pull her out so we had to use the pickup. That horse ended up being used for team roping.

I had a horse that was green broke, and Warner wanted me to use him to lead the stud out to the stud pasture. I didn't have a long enough lead rope, and the stud jerked away from me. He got loose, and I and the green-broke horse were chasing him back to the barn. My horse stumbled with both front feet and did a complete somersault. I looked up and all I could see was his rear end and his tail sticking straight in the air. Luckily, he came down on his back right beside me, landed, and then rolled right on top of me. I hit him in the face with my hand. He got up, but he had knocked the air out of me. I lay there and got my air back, then hobbled back into the house after unsaddling the horse. I took it pretty easy for a little while. I can still see the image of that horse's rear and tail in the air above me. What a helpless feeling!

Warner had three studs at his place. One called King was a King-P234 horse. He was a direct son of King, a King Ranch horse from Texas. That was an excellent line, and the colts were heavily muscled and a little on the hot side. He had a Depth Charge stud, another top line. I loved most of the colts out of him – they were tall, thoroughbred-type, with good dispositions. I broke one four-year-old gelding, and the guy who bought him used him as a ranch horse and a team-roping horse and really liked him.

The third stud was Flying Sox. Rancher Harold Atkins had said earlier he was probably the best quarter-horse stud in the country, but I learned to disagree! I don't remember that stud's pedigree. Most every colt was crooked-legged with a sour disposition. I kept a mare named Rose from Flying Sox, and she was crooked-legged and mostly wanted to buck, including when I tried to team rope with her. I was trying to impress Cherie in those days, and getting nearly bucked off when you're trying to come out of the team roping chute isn't exactly impressive! I got Rose bred and then sold her. This is a good time to comment that learning to be a good judge of horses as well as a good rider and trainer takes plenty of time and experience, and some of it is not easy!

High Pockets was Warner Johnson's main saddle horse. He was 16 ½ hands tall, a quarter horse with some thoroughbred, which sometimes produces a tall, rangy horse. He was just a good traveling horse. The neighbors came over at calving time, and they had a cow that needed a calf pulled. She got into Warner's bunch. I was riding High Pockets and roped her, turned the other way, and jerked her down. Warner and neighbor Brad tied her down and pulled the calf. Warner told Brad, "You pet her nice, then get those ropes off her," and she chased them both back to the flatbed pickup. We got quite a laugh out of that.

CHAPTER 8

PARDNER

This is probably the saddest chapter you are going to read in this book. People who love animals like horses learn early on that most humans are going to outlive most animals. It's just a fact of life. But that doesn't make the times of outliving them easy, and my time with Pardner is especially one of those times.

Pardner was a very special horse. I broke him for neighbor Clarence Olson and when I returned him, they didn't ride him for a long time. When Clarence's brother Harry went to ride him, he was raring and acting goofy. They wanted to sell him, and I bought him. I just saddled him up and went to riding him. He wanted to "come home." He was a brown horse, not as tall as Shane, and quite a bit stockier.

Pardner was a good traveling horse, a decent rope horse, worked cattle well, and was always willing for whatever I wanted to do. He wanted to work. In fact, if I took another horse in the morning Pardner would stand there by the corral fence and look disappointed. I used him for team roping as well as ranch work. He wasn't particularly fast but he sure would take off when asked.

There are not a lot of horses who truly earn a name and reputation as "Pardner." My wife was used to me coming in the house singing Pardner's praises for the day's work. My brother and I in the process of expanding our operation saved replacement heifers and did more cowboying. Pardner was the best horse for the job. I don't have a lot of Pardner stories. If you get a horse that good, you aren't going to have a lot of wrecks or mishaps with him. He just does his job. You can see him in the picture at the beginning of this book; I picked that picture because I never had a better pardner.

We were at a branding on the Redwater River, and I was using Pardner. At dinner time, I made a halter out of a lariat rope, tied it to a tree, and left it long so he could graze. He stepped on the tail of the rope, threw his head up, broke his neck, and died. I found him there and could hardly believe it. I helped the neighbor bury him. It took me a long time to get over it. Sometimes it seems to me that when you have something you really like, something happens. Sorry SOBs can be around forever. But Pardner was one of many lessons I've learned about valuing horses and people for whatever time you have, realizing that good memories and good pictures, both printed and mental, can keep them close forever.

CHAPTER 9

COMANCHE

Another favorite horse was Comanche. He was out of Canfields' Ignition stud, a blue roan. Blue roans have a black base coloring with a sprinkling of white hairs which makes the coat appear grayish-blue. They are beautiful animals, but this is a good time to mention that unless a horse is being used as part of a team or a group, like the Shriners' Black Horse Patrol or the Palomino Drill Team who open the San Antonio Rodeo, color is not a trait I look for when selecting horses. A plain old brown horse can be the best horse you own, even if he could never be a show horse. Remember my story about our daughter Anne using Shane as a 4-H show horse? That sure wasn't for looks; it was for his response to her and his performance in the ring.

I bought Comanche as a three-year-old and broke him. When we moved away from the home place, we took him and Shane. I used Comanche for a lot of years. When we lived near Harlowton, I was working for a cattle buyer named Byron Berg, and he had a whole rash of pink eye in cattle. I used Comanche a lot for that job, depending on his cattle sense, calmness during roping, and endurance to rope and treat the cattle. In that country there were days when I had to run the cattle with the wind; otherwise, I would throw a loop and it would come right back at me!

I moved a lot of cattle on Comanche. I used him on a forest permit in the Snowy Mountains. That area had a lot of bears. One time I was riding back from putting out salt, and the horse wouldn't go on down the trail past a big bush. I tried several times and finally had to go way around. I'm sure there was a bear in the bush, and horses sure can sense them.

My oldest boy Clint had learned to ride with a pony but graduated to Comanche when he was about a third grader. He did well with Comanche, but one day we were trailing cattle in the

Careless Creek area near where Charlie Russell's "Bronc to Breakfast" was painted. Clint was daydreaming and rode right into an open gate where the barbed wire was lying on the ground. Comanche got caught in the barbed wire and stood perfectly still. I lifted his leg over the wire and then led him out of there with a very scared kid on his back. If Comanche had reacted by thrashing around, that story could have had a very different outcome. I admired Clint that day because he went right back to riding, learned his lesson, and took another step toward being a good hand.

Comanche was one of those ranch horses you can really depend on. He had speed when I needed it and was sensible when I needed that. I used him for team roping, and Clint continued to ride and enjoy him for moving cattle and other ranch work. We moved Comanche with us to Broadus and then Rosebud. When he was about 14 years old, he developed ring bone; it's a joint problem where the bone below the hairline gets damaged and lames the horse up. He had to be sold, and I sure missed him.

Clint on Comanche, Anne on Princess, Josh on Blackie, Doug on a Berg mare

Ribbons at the Wheatland County Fair: Josh and Anne with Blackie, Clint with Comanche

CHAPTER 10

KIDS AND HORSES

Before I talk about our kids' first horses, I need to share my two cents in general about kids and horses. I have always loved both. When our kids were teenagers, a woman commented that she felt for anybody raising teenagers because it was so difficult. My wife and I were both surprised because even though we acknowledged that it wasn't always a walk in the park, raising teenagers wasn't that bad in the long run. I told the woman, "Raising teenagers is a lot like training young horses. You need a firm hand and a gentle touch."

Horses are a wonderful thing for kids, beginning quite young, but I need to stress that a parent needs to know something about horses and be willing to stay on top of things if a kid is going to make any kind of a rider. The first thing is to pick the right horse. The idea of putting a kid on a young, green horse and having them "grow up together" is mostly destined for trouble. Older, dependable horses are fine as long as you remember that young kids are going to have to learn on a larger saddle than might fit them well and that on a full-sized horse, a kid is looking a long way down to the ground!

For that reason, ponies with smaller kids' saddles are great, as long as you pick the right one. A Shetland pony seems to be the worst for being spoiled and doing whatever he chooses rather than having any awareness of what the kid on his back wants him to do. There are exceptions to that comment about Shetlands, of course, but I prefer Welsh ponies.

Of course, very young children need to be on a horse in front of someone older or held by someone walking alongside while they are sitting on a horse on their own. With supervision, even quite young children can become proficient quickly with the right instruction. Most important is the concept that the kid needs to be the one in charge. He's not just "dummying along" and letting the horse make all the choices but instead is actually riding with authority. Kids should always practice in a corral and should work on turns and different speeds until they get the hang of it enough to ride outside the corral.

Let's talk about learning styles, something school teachers know all about and something adults working with kids in all sports should know about, too. Many people are visual learners. They are the ones who read or see by example what to do. Many others are auditory learners. They are the ones who need to listen, who can be told, sometimes repeatedly, what to do. However, a small part of the population are kinesthetic learners, which means they learn best by doing and by bodily awareness of what is right. Our youngest son Josh, who struggled with a dyslexic learning disability, was a kinesthetic learner. He was highly observant, but he needed to be taught in a way that made him aware of how things should be handled and how they should feel.

A good example of what I am talking about happened when Josh needed to learn to side pass, a horsemanship skill necessary for things like Trail Class in 4-H. In side passing, a horse moves his feet in a way to keep him moving straight sideways instead of forward or backward. It's easier said than done! But I just worked with Josh on his 4-H horse Eagle and me on one of the other horses, making him aware of when to press with a knee, when to guide with the reins, and how to make the horse aware that he was doing the maneuver right. All of that is kinesthetic learning, and unlike one basketball coach who stood on the sidelines and yelled at our 6'8" son with no positive effect, I could teach Josh in a way that fit his learning style.

The biggest thing I'll say about training young riders — and all three of our kids got to be excellent riders — is that they need to get some experience actually using their horses and their knowledge for something practical. Riding around corrals or around pastures or down the road is fine, but using a horse to get somewhere, to ride different terrains, to move cattle, and eventually to add skills like roping will yield far better results in the long run.

In her later high school years and beyond, our daughter Anne joined the Rosebud Sidesaddlers. She adapted quickly to a sidesaddle, and she and Hank were part of many parades and Fair Rodeo performances with the group. Imagine sitting poised in a long dress on a saddle that demands perfect balance; then imagine loping and jumping over hay bales! She and Hank did it without a glitch, and her horsemanship benefited.

Furthermore, working with horses overcomes the boredom that can take over if the riding is just riding. Our kids have always joked about my getting them to saddle up before dawn and then talk about "burning daylight" if we weren't well on our way. However, those days in their child and teen years when they were saddled up and really doing something on horses made a tremendous difference in the progress toward the talented riders they became.

I will never forget one branding day at the Newman Place north of the tiny burg of Ingomar, Montana. All three kids were with me, and we rode a ways into a large grazing district pasture and dealt with a sticky situation where our cows and calves were mixed with other ranchers' cows. My kids and I worked together like a well-oiled machine, sorting, gathering, and moving those cattle. We were bringing up calves from behind and occasionally correcting the lead cattle so they wouldn't stray into the wrong areas.

The sun made the sage smell strong, the warmth was comfortable on my shoulders, and the warmth around my heart watching my three efficient young riders has stayed with me as a mental image all these years.

That practical knowledge and horsemanship has continued into their adult years. I never tire of getting a chance to ride with a kid or grandkid. I could call up my older son or daughter today and ask for help with cows, and either one of them would slip into the saddle with confidence and be right back where they were for so many adventures. Even better, they would be smiling.

Clint on Comanche, Josh on Blackie, Anne on Princess, Doug on the hill on a Berg mare

CHAPTER 11

BLACKIE AND PRINCESS

My Harlowton and Judith Gap country boss, Byron Berg, returned from a Billings cattle sale one day with a Welsh pony he bought through the ring. He unloaded the pony in our yard for the kids. Blackie was a beautiful pony and very good with the kids. I remember Clint's first ride on her; he was about four years old. Blackie jumped a small irrigation ditch and Clint rolled off the back end. He came strutting back toward the house, wet and muddy and just so proud of himself, saying "Buck off!" All three of the kids learned to ride on Blackie.

Blackie was at the center of one of my most embarrassing stories. One winter we had a bunch of calves, and they managed to knock down a pile of corral poles I was working with. One pole caught Blackie on a hind leg and dislocated her ankle. The vet put her in a cast and said she shouldn't be used for a while. During the winter, Blackie gained weight, and I told the kids they would really have to use her in the spring to take those extra pounds off. One morning I went out to check for lambs, and there was a foal on the ground! I've been around horses all my life, but I sure missed that pregnancy, partly because she didn't bag up much. Anyhow, I called Byron and asked him if he wanted to go partners!

Doug on Princess, 1983

As a result of all this, the kids had two ponies. Our daughter Anne named the foal Princess. I rode her enough to get her broke, and the kids still chuckle over the picture of me on two-year-old Princess with my boots almost touching the ground. Princess broke well and made a great kids' horse. One day we were all on horseback, including three-year-old Josh on Blackie, five-year-old Anne on Princess, seven-year-old Clint on Comanche, and Cherie and me on Berg horses.

We came around the side of a hill, and there was a mother antelope giving birth to a second kid. We stood there, with our kids and the horses silent at my gesture, and watched that birth and the mother getting the pair of antelope kids to their feet. Then we silently rode away, with the kids just amazed at what they had seen. What an education!

When we left Judith Gap, Blackie had to be put to sleep because of heaves, a horse disease much like asthma which really weakens the lungs. Josh accepted that we had to leave Blackie behind when we moved. Kids' education related to horses goes far beyond learning to ride and includes understanding health and body conditions and loss.

After we moved to Rosebud, Anne used Princess as a 4-H horse. She and Princess did lead changes during Horsemanship I (above the level of that class) and won the purple rosette. Princess had good legs and feet and stood up on her feet so pretty. She was an honest horse, very responsive and willing with very little of the typical pony trait of acting spoiled and difficult. Anne used Princess for several years and outgrew her, and by then Princess had a colt. It was time to let some other kids have good ponies and we sold Princess and the colt.

My big old gelding Shane had adopted that colt and looked after it in the pasture. When the pair were sold, loaded into a horse trailer, and headed west, Shane stood looking down the road toward where the colt had gone. He never left that corner by the gate for several days, just gazing down the road. A person gets to know a lot about horses just by working with them every day, but every now and then something like that will just strike you with the understanding of what social and loving animals horses can be.

CHAPTER 12

SOCKS

Socks was raised by Dick Cheesum, who could be a whole chapter in this book! I bought Socks from a friend as a green-broke horse. He had four white feet, thus his name, and was a blaze-faced sorrel. Socks was probably one of the toughest horses I've ever ridden. He could go and go and go. He also was really high-strung. I had to use a bosal on him, a kind of hackamore used for breaking horses because a bit made him nervous and he would fight it. I rode him most of the time with the bosal. I used him any time we had a long ride to gather cattle or work them partly because he had such endurance and partly because he needed the first part of the ride to get his nerves settled down.

We were at the Smith Place up in the hills southeast of Rosebud. Clint shot off a rifle for target practice just as I stepped on Socks. It spooked the horse, and he went to bucking. He tore into it and bucked toward a reservoir. He unloaded me at the water's edge so I got muddy, and he kept bucking right straight through the reservoir. We got him caught, and he was fine. Once the kids and Cherie saw I was okay, they sure got a laugh out of it. It wasn't often I got piled or ended up muddy.

Socks got to be a pretty fair cowhorse and was fine for heeling calves around branding fires and wrestlers, which says he had mellowed a lot, although that could vary. The funniest story about Socks happened another time when we were up on the Smith Place. A rancher let some pigs loose to graze when feed was expensive. We came on a few pigs, and Socks just turned inside out. He didn't buck me off, but he sure spooked and spooked. Josh and his horse just went on with the job of checking on cattle and ignored Socks' tantrum.

Like so many of my good horses, Socks got used from the time he was young into his late adulthood. When Socks got a little older, one of his feet split all the way to the hairline. I kept him shod, but it didn't heal, and I had to sell him. He is another example of the jeopardy of foot and leg problems which are always a risk for horses.

Doug on Socks trailing to the Smith Place, summer of 1989

CHAPTER 13

ROANIE AND OTHER HARSTAD HORSES

Roanie, as his name implies, was a red roan, and I acquired him when he was four or five. Rancher John Harstad, another rancher I worked for, bought him through a Billings sale for a saddle horse. We were riding down on the Northern Cheyenne Reservation, trying to get some cattle out of John's permit. I ran a bull by John, and he hit Roanie with his spurs. The horse bucked him off. John was in his late 70s and we were a long way from the pickup. I was never so glad to see an old feller get up in my life! Two weeks later John had a heart attack and died. His family was trying to eliminate some of John's horses, so they sold Roanie to me.

Roanie did have a tendency to buck. He was really a good cow-working horse, and if you took down your rope, you may as well have thrown your bridle away, because he was after the target! However, if things didn't go right, he would bog his head and buck hard for about four jumps. After that, he would settle back down fine. Again, Roanie is an example of why it pays to ride a horse a lot and really get to know him. If things went south, I was ready for Roanie to throw his fit, knowing it wouldn't last long and I would have a good horse under me for the rest of that job.

One of the funniest branding stories happened when we were branding for a rancher named Ray Batey who ran Charolais cattle, a large breed. I was riding Roanie for roping and dragging calves in to be branded. I noticed one big Charolais calf who was looking things over and obviously going to make a break for it. I went to rope him, and when the rope touched his legs, he took off like a shot right through the branding fire, knocking things over and running over a couple of wrestlers. I had managed to double hock the calf and dally (rope two legs and get the rope secure around the saddle horn). That meant that when he hit the end of the rope, I could drag him back through to where a couple of wrestlers could get him down. We got him branded, and Roanie got a lot of credit for helping me. Thank goodness for a stout horse!

One time we were dealing with calves that had run back instead of going through a gate. We gathered them and forced them through. When the last calf was through the gate, Roanie just had to throw a fit. Then he was fine again. I used him on the Harstad Ranch and then on the Montgomery Ranch. My oldest son Clint rode him, but whenever he started to buck, Clint just stepped off. Roanie was pretty predictable, and Clint knew him well enough to be prepared.

He was riding Roanie one time, and they got the cows gathered. The cows were milling around, and Clint was doing his best to hold them. One cow came out of the bunch and hit Roanie right square in the chest. The horse braced himself and took it pretty well. Then the cow hit him again, and Roanie reared up and hit the cow over the head with both front feet and knocked her down. Clint was just along for that Lone Ranger ride! The cow got up and sidled back into the bunch, and Roanie just went back to business. I imagine Clint heaved a sigh of relief.

Roanie was light-boned and developed foot problems, and I had to sell him. Feet and legs are the most vulnerable parts of horses, especially quarter horses, who are usually light-boned. They either break bones in their feet or develop ring bone. It's a bony growth that develops right along the hairline above the hoof. It makes the foot sore to flex, and they end up lame. Horses get stiffer as they age, are not as flexible, and can develop joint problems, but mostly they end up with foot problems.

Doug roping on Roanie, branding at Verner Carlson's place south of
Miles City, 1997

Much of the time at the Harstad Ranch I worked with John's son-in-law Tiny Ottun, who was an excellent horseman and ran a lot of young horses for futurities. Tiny had a horse named Pete who was fun to ride. We roped a lot of calves on him to ear tag and doctor scours, a dangerous diarrhea-type disease that spreads when calves are together. Pete could really run, and he was a reckless bugger. Slippery ground didn't bother him one bit. Tiny's daughter Jaime was riding him one time, chasing a calf that turned on one of the wet hard-pan spots. The calf slipped and fell down, and Pete turned right with him and kept his feet. All I could do was hold my breath! They let me ride Pete quite a little, and I loved it.

Tiny raised two or three colts every year. When they got to be two or three years old, he would use them for futurity barrel racing. He was raising this one filly, and she was pretty green. He went to the calving pasture to tag a calf and got the calf roped in the creek. The calf ran under the horse's belly, and Tiny wouldn't let go of the rope. It took a pretty good horse to unload Tiny, but that horse bucked him off into the creek.

I was feeding with the pickup and came over the hill to see a horse running for home, a calf running the other way, and Tiny coming out of the creek soaking wet. The steam was just rolling off him he was so mad! He kept riding her, but all she wanted to do was buck, so he sold her to Newman Rodeo Company.

Another story involving Tiny happened one wintry day when we were gathering cattle out of the Buttes, a rough badland-y area south of Rosebud. Tiny always wanted us to split up when we were gathering; he would look at two men riding along beside each other and jest, "Those guys must be riding one horse." Anyhow, I was riding a smaller pinto horse alone, following two young cows who started climbing up the sides of a steep badland area.

People who cowboy regularly in the badlands get wise to the fact that they are incredibly slippery when wet, just like a bar of soap. When the cows continued to climb to the very top, I got off my horse and tied him by the reins to a tree so that I could continue on foot. Normally, I won't tie a horse by the reins – a halter is a much better, less breakable choice – but this was a special situation.

I climbed up and circled around behind the cows and started hazing them downhill. The main concern going through my head was having the young cows bolt and spook the horse. If he reared up and broke the reins, I could be afoot in that large, rough area. As it turned out, the cattle ran past the horse but he very sensibly stayed where he was. I was mighty relieved to untie the reins and continue making my way behind the cows, headed for the other bunch being gathered. Part of what a person is looking for, both in horses and in fellow riders, is just what that horse had: common sense.

45

CHAPTER 14

EAGLE

Ralph Nybol from south of Miles City raised Eagle, a blaze-faced sorrel who was a Three Bars horse, until a rancher I was running cattle with named Van Blankenship bought Eagle as a colt. I haven't said a lot about horse lines like Three Bars because I have always been more interested in how a horse trains and acts than his bloodlines. However, sometimes bloodlines carry traits either desirable or not desirable in the colts, all the way from conformation to character. The Three Bars horses were bred for quarter horse race horses, a whole different part of the horse industry than the thoroughbred race horses you hear about at Kentucky Derby time. In addition to their speed, they acquire from their famous sire an easy-going temperament.

I broke Eagle the summer when he was three, and he was used for riding the pipeline on Van's place. We were coming back – a long ride – and all of sudden, Eagle bucked me off. He could have been bumped by one of the rancher's dogs. After that, he wanted to buck pretty regularly. Then one day Eagle stepped on a big cactus, which broke off, flipped up, and hit him in the butt. A friend riding with me moved his horse in front of Eagle -- kind of a Mexican standoff -- and Eagle settled down. He never offered to buck again after that. I finished breaking him that winter, and then Van gave the horse to eight-year-old Josh because the kid was such a good rider and so crazy about Eagle. It was a horse-and-rider relationship which lasted the rest of their lives.

The next spring included one of the most demanding, challenging horseback riding days I have ever experienced, and it happened with four-year-old green-broke Eagle. I have mentioned Dick Cheesum and how he could be a whole chapter; well, here goes! My long-time boss Kent Montgomery had rented a huge 29-section pasture on Ryan's Fork north of Forsyth, and this story takes place the first time I ever saw that pasture, which has become a major part of my horseback-riding life.

It had been a rough winter, and the spring started out warmer and plenty muddy. A friend and fellow cowboy named Jim Chandler and his wife went for a Sunday drive on the back road by that pasture and noticed a bunch of horses there. Jim knew they weren't Kent's and told Kent about them. When Kent flew over the pasture, about 100 horses were scattered around that area, and he and the pilot could read Dick Cheesum's brand on several horses. He called Dick and they assembled a crew of 11 riders including me for the roundup.

We gathered horses for half a day through that rough country, and the spring mud was a real challenge. The horse band, which had been up there since December, was well familiar with where to run and hide. A teenage girl on a stout horse and I on young Eagle gathered up a bunch of the horses into the northeast corner of the pasture and could see another bunch being moved across the way. We pushed our bunch that way and finally got the horses all together.

As a four-year-old, Eagle had proved himself to be an excellent endurance horse, but the mud was deep and he finally played out. I got off and led him for a while. Eventually, we all got the horses corralled at the Rolston Place, the first time I saw that part of the country as well. We got all but a few mares with colts, and a week later we went back, with me on Eagle again, and got the last of them. The funny part is that Dick just ended up with a $2,000 fine, which is cheap pasture rent for 100 horses for four months! Eventually, Kent bought that pasture. I have spent a lot of time riding in the Ryan's Fork area, but I never had another adventure quite that exciting.

Josh was just nine years old the next spring when he began riding Eagle regularly. The first ride Josh made on Eagle was trailing from Van's place to the Smith place, about 10 miles, and they got along well. After that, Josh and Eagle were inseparable. Josh started 4-H that year and used Eagle for many 4-H years.

Cherie remembers so well the first win by Josh and Eagle. She was working the photography booth at the Fair and feeling bad about missing Josh's first Horsemanship I class. Then she noticed a hand circling around the pillar at the edge of the booth, holding a pink Reserve Champion rosette. Next came Josh's head peeking around and a big grin. Of course, he got a hearty congratulations.

This is a good time to mention a bit more of our philosophy about raising kids and horses. As I have mentioned, Josh had a learning disability related to dyslexia, and reading and writing were a real challenge. He struggled through school and at times resented other kids having an easy time. We knew that the way to ease such a challenge is to make sure that a kid has another way in which they can excel. The answer for Josh was competing and often winning on Eagle, and we have credited the horse as a major part of Josh's graduating from high school.

By age 11, Josh was doing not only Horsemanship classes but also Western Pleasure, Reining, and Showmanship, with Josh winning and being part of the Round Robin. One funny picture of the two of them came when they were waiting in line for quite a while to compete in Horsemanship. The other kids were pretty nervy, sitting impatiently atop fidgety horses. Then there was Josh, leaning back in the saddle with both legs on one side of Eagle's neck, and both of them just as laid-back as they could be. When the time came to get down to business, they won the class.

Eagle was the ultimate Western Pleasure horse in a class that demanded smooth riding, turning, and maneuvers with a rider always in control. One year so many Junior-level 4-H kids were entered in Western Pleasure that the judge had to run three different groups and then take the top kids from each group and narrow it down to a few blue-ribbon winners to compete for the top prizes. In 100-degree heat, Josh and Eagle performed three times, waiting quietly between each performance. At the end of the class, Josh and Eagle had earned Grand Champion. His grin made every minute worth it.

Despite all the use for 4-H, Eagle never liked being stalled at the Fairgrounds amid other horses and riders and the public viewers. Shane loved the whole experience, but Eagle didn't and tended to sour after a few days. One time Eagle was outside his stall and the kids' friend Clay walked by with a colt. Suddenly Eagle kicked and hit Clay square, luckily on his big belt buckle so it just knocked the wind out of him. When the horse classes were done and riders were allowed to take some horses home, I gathered up Josh and Eagle, both of whom had had enough of the Fair, and took them home. That afternoon was the subject of a favorite poem of Cherie's.

THE BOY AND HIS HORSE

The boots are polished, shiny and bright,
Pants are creased and shirt pressed fine
The horse is groomed, glowing and sleek,
Showing head to hooves with satin shine.

The boy, too, is slicked up and ready,
Hat just right and shoulders straight.
Every inch the well-trained showman
Confidently entering the gate.

With ease they ride the pattern's guide,
Now walk, now trot, now smoothly lope,
Side pass, roll back, pivot and turn,
Give the judge a glance of hope.

They wait with mute anticipation;
The trial is over, the rosette is won.
With mutual pride, both boy and horse
Glow once more, the job well done.

The fine clothes finally are tossed aside;
Old jeans and shirt can take their place,
An aging hat over hair less combed
Matches scuffed boots pulled on in haste.

The horse, too, can roll and stretch
And lose the gleam from coat and mane.
Together they seek the grassy hills,
With freedom filling hearts again.

They run, and the wind runs at their side
And a lazy hawk adorns the sky.
Here they are one, with ease and grace,
Though far from the judge's watchful eye.

C.J. Heser

Josh heeled a lot of calves on Eagle, helped trail a lot of cows, and helped with a lot of brandings. As a former teacher, Cherie has to confess that when spring came and Josh was getting restless and tired of trying in school, she would get him out of school within the allotted number of missed days. Then he and Eagle were free to help with the neighborhood brandings as long as Josh got his schoolwork taken care of. He and Eagle were always outstanding together and, as I have emphasized, very much in tune. They were depended on by ranchers, and that continued into adulthood.

Josh hadn't been riding Eagle very long when I had the kids with me in a big grazing area and wanted to go a separate way. I told Josh, "You remember where we killed that rattlesnake?" He did. When I got to that spot, there sat Josh under a tree with Eagle grazing. The other kids had gone elsewhere looking for me, but Josh and Eagle were just where they belonged.

Eagle continued as a useful saddle horse for many years, and we have many pictures of Josh with little nephews and nieces on Eagle, either sitting in front of him on the horse or perched on his back with Josh leading. At home, Eagle was an alpha horse who definitely ruled the roost and the hay manger at our place.

Josh died young, and we have a treasured picture of him the weekend before he died, posed with both Eagle and Josh's new horse, Tucker. With Josh's arm over his neck, Eagle forgot to be cranky and accepted Tucker standing there nearby. Eagle lived to be 29 years old. And yeah, there were times in those last years he would stand looking off down the road, and I was sure I knew what he was thinking and feeling.

Our treasured last picture of Josh with me, Tucker, and Eagle, October 2013

CHAPTER 15

HANK

Anne with Hank at the Rosebud-Treasure County Fairgrounds

Our daughter Anne, also an outstanding rider and hand, wanted a horse for the yearling through five-year-old 4-H project, which involves competing each year of the horse's growth. Anne and I went to Winnett, Montana, and picked through a bunch of Larry Grantier's stud colts. We bought Hank Buck Jay, a buckskin weanling whom Anne quickly named Hank. We halter broke him through the winter, and Anne started with him as a yearling. She did a lot of work with him to teach him to walk, trot, and jog at a lead, pick up his feet, and set up with all four feet even. It was a challenge because Hank was a slow-maturing horse with an ornery, mischievous streak that stayed with him all his life.

That summer Anne took her well-trained horse to the Rosebud-Treasure County Fair to compete in the Yearling Class, the first class in several days' competitions. Anne was dressed in the immaculate white shirt and black jeans required in those years for horse classes. Just before they entered the ring, Hank grabbed a clump of green grass and then proceeded to nibble on Anne's white shirt sleeve and leave green stains that disgusted his rider. They proceeded into the ring, and Hank discovered that he was on display with a whole bunch of other young horses and owners. He forgot everything he had learned. He fidgeted, refused to set up, resisted when she tried to turn him around to try again at setting up, wouldn't lead for walking or jogging, and so on.

When the ordeal was over, Anne had a lowly white ribbon, something which didn't sit well with her competitive nature, and we could see the tears in her eyes and the storm coming which could be a challenge and threaten to spoil her Fair experience. She took Hank's lead rope and the white ribbon and started dejectedly walking out of the ring. Hank reached down, grabbed that white ribbon in his mouth, and ate it! Anne busted out laughing, and that ended the whole ordeal. She and Hank did fine from that point on.

I had the vet cut Hank, making him a gelding in his two-year-old year. That summer Anne broke him to ride and rode him a lot with me. One time after we took off at a gallop, I looked back, and Anne was riding a bucking horse! Hank managed to buck her off. She got back on and we slowed things down a bit. She was a trooper and handled it well. At the Fair that year, she and Hank did better in both Horsemanship and Showmanship. She won many blue ribbons and Grand Champion and Reserve Champion rosettes in very competitive classes with him through her senior year.

As a three-year-old, Hank was Anne's mount while we helped the Porcupine Ranch gather their heifers out of the Rattlesnake Pasture. We were sorting spayed heifers from breeding heifers. We had them held up along the fence, and one quit the bunch. Anne took off after her, and Hank ran right past the heifer. Anne yanked Hank around, lined him out, and brought the heifer back at a dead run. Bruce Kreutzer was running the show, and when he saw that happen, I thought he was going to fall off his horse laughing.

Hank was a smooth gaited horse and very good at reining. She continued to work hard with him, and he learned more advanced moves like side passing. The next adventure came when Anne was invited to be part of the Rosebud Sidesaddlers, a group of ladies from Forsyth and Rosebud ranging from teenagers like Anne to elderly women like Ruth Watson, who rode sidesaddle into her 90s. Anne and Hank were impressive with sidesaddle and rode in parades and performed at half times at the county fair. Hank could jump hay bales with his rider firmly in her sidesaddle seat!

Anne became quite a hand, and Hank needed a rider with a firm hand. He remained coltish all his life. He was a horse who should have had one of those big play balls which are now popular with some horse owners. When Hank was in winter pasture, he would get bored and just be mischievous. He managed to pull down a bunch of hay. I was constantly adding more boards to the building above and around the feeders, trying to keep him from snaking his neck and head through to pull down more hay. Hank was always chewing on something -- his rider's pockets or the stirrups or whatever. He was always into things and getting cut up. The final time, he got into wire and cut some tendons, which crippled him. Anne came home from Missoula and said goodbye to Hank before we had him put down.

With Josh on Eagle, Anne on Hank, Clint on Shane, and me on Socks or Pretty Boy, we moved a lot of cattle and did a lot of practical cattle work. I loved that time with the kids and they loved it, too, although they always laugh about saddling up in the dark and me commenting about "wasting daylight." Josh and Anne both at different times in their lives came home and rode with me to heal up from difficulties and sadness. Clint has helped me a number of times, and it has been fun having his boys join in the riding at branding time. Riding has always been a combination of work and fun for me. It's a challenge that is fun to meet, especially with yearlings. It always lifts my spirits.

CHAPTER 16

PRETTY BOY

Pretty boy was born a Montgomery horse. We were branding the colts, and I looked over this one kind of ugly colt and commented, "That's a pretty good horse." Kent Montgomery said, "If you can use him, I'll give him to you." He actually was a sorrel horse of good conformation, fairly tall and stoutly built. I gave him the name Pretty Boy for fun, took him home and halter broke him, then broke him as a three-year-old and used him a lot.

When he was still a colt, I brought dinner down from the camp when Kent and crew were trailing cattle up. I saddled up Pretty Boy and went out to meet them. I got up on a knoll, and a bunch of cattle were coming. Pretty Boy jumped one way and then jumped the other way, whirled around, and started to leave – and not in slow motion! We got things under control, met the bunch, and got along fine after that. I told Kent, "I didn't know whether I was going to help you or not," and Kent sure laughed.

As an adult horse, Pretty Boy could really run, and I could use him for running horses. One year we cut studs on him. We headed and heeled them to stretch them out, and he was totally reliable for that. He also was a good horse at the branding fire. One time we were trailing a stud, some mares, and baby colts to the corral at the Rolston Place north of the ranch camp where I spent so many years. Someone didn't get the gate open in time, and the stud ran back to the barn and the mares took off. Pretty Boy built to it, got them turned and headed back to the corral. I could just imagine Kent thinking, "I raised that colt."

At our place, my son Clint was shutting the gate, and Pretty Boy kicked him right in the chest with both hind feet. Clint dented up a feed bucket beating on him and never liked him after that. My wife agreed after Pretty Boy knocked her down when she was trying to feed with feed pans for him and a couple of other horses.

Cherie had another adventure with him. One spring day she was leaving home for town and discovered Pretty Boy with his leg caught down in our cattle guard. He was thrashing around so she couldn't get close; she went to the house and called the neighbors for help. When she returned to the cattle guard, Pretty Boy was gone, and she discovered him south on the hill, uninjured. Evidently, he stopped struggling and figured out a way to pull his leg out. It takes an intelligent horse to do that.

Pretty Boy was always tight when we left, a little inclined to buck but never did. He was alert and willing to work. Once after a day of branding, we were trotting home from Dog Creek. He was sulking along and stepped into a hole and fell, jabbing my elbow into the ground. That was the biggest wreck I ever had with him. If he didn't want to do something, he would sure trot hard and make every step a trial. He had that temperamental side, but all in all, he was a good horse.

I used Pretty Boy as a ranch horse for several years. At about 11 years of age, he broke a leg, and the broken bone cut an artery and ended his life. On a side note, Pretty Boy and his full brother are an example of how much sibling horses can vary. The brother was high-strung and never trustworthy. I was riding him when a rabbit jumped out, and he bucked until I lost my hat. Our group went on and took care of the cattle.

We were riding back in the Rough Creek pasture just north of the camp when all of a sudden, he tore into it again. He bogged his head and went to bucking in a circle. He bucked into my friend Jim's horse, and that saved my bacon, stopping him long enough for me to get squared up on him. Kent said, "You're too valuable a man to be riding that horse," and after that, they assigned him to another hand, who got bucked off several times. Then a neighbor tried to work with him and just about quit breaking horses over that experience!

CHAPTER 17

TOM

Tom was a High Rollin' Roany colt. It's worth saying something about that line. The legendary horse High Rolling Roany was a roan stallion with a blend of Driftwood, Hancock, and Three Bars, "as good a horse to ride as you could ask for" according to the American Quarter Horse Association. Tom sure proved he was a descendant.

Kent Montgomery bought Tom for a stud. When he got to be a three-year-old, Kent decided Tom was going to throw colts too big for him and his son to get on, so he cut him. That summer my son Josh broke him. Kent sold Tom to me, and he was good for everything until he was a really old horse. When he was a colt, you just saddled him up and left. He didn't want to be messed with bridle-wise or tack-wise, just go and kick some miles behind him.

Tom is a classic example of what I look for in the way of disposition for a good saddle horse. It's a little hard to explain. I want obedience, submission, and willingness to be trained. At the same time, I want intelligence and a horse who has cow sense, common sense, and the ability to be a partner in cowboying tasks. Tom was that kind of horse.

As an adult horse, he was 16 hands, a handsome red roan. He was an excellent cowhorse; in all my experience, only Shane was better with cattle. As Tom got a little older, especially gathering bulls, he would only put up with so much hassle. If they were wanting to break away, he would dive in and bite them. There were times he could scare you. If you weren't paying attention, he could turn right out from under you. When he got older and was being used to rope for branding, if the wrestlers didn't get the calf down right away, Tom absolutely would not pull the calf any farther.

The biggest scare I ever got with Tom was when we were gathering bulls and had one that was kind of feisty. We had him with a bunch of cows and tried to turn the cows back. The bull whirled and hit Tom right under his flank. Tom just stood there and went to biting the bull. The bull backed off and started the right way. I took Tom back to get the cows rather than deal with that bull any further. Tom was completely cool about the whole thing.

One time Clint was riding Tom to gather bulls. Tom built to a bull and went to biting on him. He was pressing so hard on the bull that Clint thought he was going to end up with a broken leg. When the bull headed the right way, Tom just backed off, and Clint gave a sigh of relief. Tom was an amazing combination of both aggressive and sensible. He was one of the best horses I ever had. He was excellent for roping, and he was really good when we were shipping cattle for running them down the lane and getting them on the scale.

Tom was a nice horse to have around. Anyone could ride him, and he wouldn't fudge on them, just do whatever needed to be done. All three of our kids rode him well. I remember one time when Annie came home from college. She stuck her foot in the stirrup at about her eye level, bounced a couple of times, and was up there. She rode Tom for miles that day and commented on how much she enjoyed him.

Tom was from the Hancock line that had a slightly crooked, flat-footed left foot. It never stopped him from running well, but it eventually broke down when he was older. Tom was 21 years old when he had to be put down. He had spent most of his life at the Radeen Place, so I decided that would be his final resting place, looking west, headed for final pastures. There are a few horses I really shed tears over, and Tom was one.

Doug on Tom and grandson Taye on Bandit, our place, August 2017

CHAPTER 18

COMET

Comet is a black horse with a white strip that looks like a comet. He was a Montgomery colt who was the biggest, ugliest colt in the bunch, so they gave him to me. Have you noticed how often I ended up with the ugly ones? Good thing I wasn't looking for beauty and instead was looking for a great saddle horse! I was getting a little long in the tooth to do the major breaking so had someone else break Comet as a three-year-old.

Comet was a horse who would buck. When he was young, I used him to put pairs out in the pasture after calving, and that really helped him settle down and learn to be cow-y. I liked to use him for dragging calves to the branding fire. When he was about five years old, he slipped in a gumbo ravine and hurt his back. I had a horse chiropractor work on him. I learned a lot that day about what the chiropractor did and about the vulnerability of spines in horses. Comet definitely improved. But from that point on he was slower and more cautious and took care of himself a little better.

Where Comet really shone was his calm attitude. He never panicked. When he was a colt, he was caught in a pile of baling twine strings. He was just standing there in a situation where a lot of horses, especially colts, would have been thrashing around and getting even more tangled up. I cut Comet loose, and he just walked off.

Just recently, as an older horse, Comet saw the neighbor's horses and put a foot over the fence between them. He stood there with his foot caught, and another neighbor saw him and got me to come. Comet continued to stand there while I cut three wires and finally got him loose. He bled a little but wasn't badly hurt. I guess if a horse is going to do something stupid and get himself into a situation like that, it helps if he's calm enough to stay sensible until things are fixed.

Another time at the camp we were moving cattle, and a calf came out of the branding corral. We ran him past the gate several times, and he ended up standing in front of the gate. Comet was still really young, and I was debating whether I wanted to rope the calf. But I did it, and we got the calf back inside. He handled that well as a really young horse who had never been used for roping calves before that.

One time the government trapper was hunting coyotes with an airplane. He landed in the Radeen Place driveway to drop off some coyotes. Comet was rolling in the dirt, and he just kept right on rolling while all this was happening. Most horses would really react to an airplane on the ground next to them! Many of them would have no tolerance for coyote smell since they are a predator that can be dangerous for horses if they're in a pack. Comet didn't even pay attention when the airplane took off.

The exception to Comet's calm attitude involved sheep. One spring I was pulling the horse trailer through a neighbor's place north of Dog Creek where there were sheep. All of a sudden, the trailer was rattling and Comet was snorting. He continued carrying on while I drove two miles beyond where the sheep were. I unloaded him, and he was still snorting and making me wonder whether I should get on. We trotted off rapidly!

The next time we had a bunch of yearlings out, I used Comet to corral them at that same neighbor's place next to where the sheep were. Comet was dancing around, whirling around, and snorting. I finally just got off and led him to the corral. I loaded him up and he finally settled down. I haven't used him around sheep since. He isn't the only horse to react to sheep that way; perhaps it's the smell or the sound, but some horses just have no tolerance for sheep.

From the time he was 10 or 12 years old, Comet had problems with teeth, a trait he inherited from his sire. That's called a "bad mouth," and I had to have his teeth floated by a veterinarian twice a year. Floating teeth involves using a drill with a disk that grinds the teeth off so that they are even. Without floating, the horse just can't chew properly, and he'll get thinner and thinner.

When I reached retirement age, I tried retiring briefly and soon realized that it just wasn't for me. So, I went back to cowboy work other than not feeding in the wintertime far from camp anymore, and I've been really glad I did.

One of my favorite stories happened when my friend and coworker Denver and I were part of a group of 11 riders gathering yearlings on Galt's Acorn Pasture way north of my camp. We separated and gathered that large pasture. Denver on Stormy and I on Comet were in the lead and got the yearlings started down a canyon when it began to snow heavily. It was actually a pretty scene with cedar trees above us. When we got to the next gate, we had to hold up and wait for the back yearlings and riders to catch up. By that time both we and the cattle were covered with snow.

I told Denver, "Why in the hell would a guy want to retire when you're having this much fun?!" He laughed so hard I thought he was going to fall off his horse. We got the yearlings moved to the Crosby Place, and the weather changed and started thawing. It was too muddy to get the pickups and trailers in, so we turned the horses loose in Brewers' State Section and hid the saddles in a coulee. Then all 11 of us piled into a Chevy Suburban and headed home. The next day we caught the horses and trailed the yearlings another 15 miles to the Rolston Camp. I was still having fun!

CHAPTER 19

BANDIT

Bandit is a pinto horse I bought from a down-and-out cowboy who got a DUI and needed $1,200 for the fine. The old fellow sure didn't want to sell him, but he trusted me to buy him and treat him well. I bought Bandit even though he was on the smaller side, something I usually wasn't looking for in a horse. But he is well built.

At first, he would run a bluff, refuse to work, and make me wonder just what I had gotten into. With a name like Bandit, what can a guy expect? But with work, he still had an attitude but would do what I needed. The more I rode him the better he got. He was good at heeling calves. My grandson Jordan learned to rope on Bandit and heeled calves for brandings. They did really well together.

Bandit turned out to be a good kid's horse. He never offered to buck, and he had a smooth ride that made things easy for kids. I have used him for regular horse work but not as much as the rest of the herd. Bandit has had a pretty easy retirement at our place. But we've got a couple of great-grandkids who are pistols and might just make Bandit earn his keep when they're a little older!

CHAPTER 20

TUCKER

Our son Josh bought Tucker as a three-year-old who had been broke but hadn't been ridden for a year. I tried to talk Josh out of buying him, considering his finances, but he went ahead, and I'm glad he did. Josh continued the training and had more fun with Tucker! He used him for helping neighbors trail cattle and brand, heel calves, and general ranch work. The first time I ever saw Tucker, Josh came down and helped me gather bulls for three days. I was so impressed by how Tucker looked and acted.

One of our favorite photos of Josh was taken at our place after we gathered the bulls. He had his old 4-H horse Eagle and Tucker as a four-year-old. He's standing there with an arm over Eagle's shoulders with Tucker standing next to the two of them, and all of them just look like they belong together. Shortly after that picture was taken, Josh died in a vehicle accident, and I bought Tucker from his widow and have used him ever since. Riding Tucker was a part of my healing from grief, and I still feel close to Josh when I use Tucker.

Tucker is one of the best-built horses I have ever owned. He is 15.3 hands, deep-bodied and well-muscled with good legs and good feet. He's a deep brown horse. The first time I headed calves on him, I could sure tell he'd done that before. I looked up at the sky and thanked Josh a couple of times. Personality-wise, he is a horse who is not going to overdo anything. But when he needs to, he can really run and really work. He doesn't really care if he gets the job done, but if I get after him, he'll sure get it done. He's good for endurance, and I can use him a couple days in a row on big jobs.

In the herd, Tucker is an alpha horse. He's always the first one in for cake or oats, and he'll sure run other horses off if he feels they are competition. He can be miserable with other horses in a corral. He'll actually herd other horses away from the water tank.

65

When he's running loose, he'll cross cattle guards and has done that in several places. We never put him in a pasture where a cattle guard is next to a county road.

One time the neighbor's dog was over bothering our horses. Tucker lowered his ears and took off after the dog, running him all the way home. If a cow isn't moving fast enough, he's willing to bite her to get her moving. When I first got Tucker, we had to trail a crippled bull to the corral. He sure didn't like trailing that slow bull and ran out of patience.

Tucker is always good on his feet and always keeps his footing. I've been in some tight spots and have been able to depend on him to get through. Tucker has never really offered to buck. He's shied and jumped sideways a few times, and as big and powerful as he is, that sideways jump can be pretty hard.

The ridge coming off the west end of the Crosby Place is pretty steep. Three of us started the yearlings down that ridge. They boiled off the ridge and then turned and headed the wrong way. I trotted Tucker off that steep part, and he fell to his knees. Being as athletic as he was, he picked himself up and continued down the bank. I was on him all that time. We got the yearlings gathered and headed back where they belonged. Tucker never hesitated.

My band of horses on our place and often all four of them up at the ranch camp are a study in contrasts. I have big, dominant Tucker, a little more of a challenge for me to get on these days but a powerful horse for riding for big jobs. Next is Ace, a little smaller and easier to get on. He, too, is dependable but in a quieter, more settled way and the subject of my next chapter. After Ace is a taller, thinner Comet, definitely aging and still having to be careful of his back but as good a horse for half-day jobs or roping jobs as any of them. Finally, the oldest and smallest horse, my pinto Bandit, stays part of the group, used a little less but always willing.

Tucker and Ace by the fence, Bandit and Comet behind, feeding. Winter 2023

CHAPTER 21

ACE

After Tom died, I needed another younger horse because Comet and Bandit were aging. Ace really fit my needs at that time. He is a smaller horse and easier for an older guy like me to get on – definitely easier than Tucker. Ace has a nice walk, a smooth gait, and is comfortable to ride. He's also good dispositioned and easy to get along with. Ace wasn't very well trained as a cattle horse but I could teach him what he needed to know.

I couldn't do things like open gates on him, but he had been used some to heel calves. Ace is a very willing horse. He reminded me of my earlier horse Pardner when he acted disgruntled because Tucker got to go in the horse trailer one day and he got left behind. He's a blood bay with a black mane, tail, and feet. Conformation-wise, he's fairly thick with good legs and feet.

I can use Ace for just about anything I need. I've used him for sorting dries and holding the herd, including keeping the cut-out dries from returning to the herd. He's not the fastest horse I've had, but he can hold his own. One of my younger grandsons rides him and ropes off him and just loves him.

We have a neighbor who has a pretty good bunch of horses and had a donkey for a while. We used to joke about how he had several horses and only one ass. My wife picked that up and kids with me every now and then for having four horses and only one ass. Seriously, however, there is a good reason for my herd of horses. For one thing, horses are very social animals. They need each other even if they pick on one another at times to establish their pecking order. A group of horses is always better located and happier. Often a horse left alone will pace, whinny a lot, and possibly try to "escape."

Most importantly, I often ride for days at a time when we are gathering and branding one bunch at a time for a week or more on the Montgomery Ranch or when we are gathering pastures, weaning, and trailing cows to winter pastures. In fairness to the horses, they are the ones carrying the weight and need days to rest. I can alternate between Tucker, Ace, and Comet, and occasionally Bandit, and always have a fresh horse. At other times, another hand or my son, daughter, or grandsons may need a horse, and I always have at least one available in addition to the one I'm using.

CHAPTER 22

OTHER HORSES I HAVE KNOWN

In the Montana Farmer-Stockman paper around 35 years ago, there was a picture where the photographer was looking forward through the ears of a horse with the comment, "Many important decisions are made with this view." I have seen that over and over. That view has become an important part of my decision-making life on ranches as well as my enjoyment of a lot of country.

My experience riding country from that perspective began with Sheep Creek and Redwater River country in northeastern Montana where I grew up. Riding several horses including colts I was breaking, I have seen a lot of that country. In rolling sandhills with numerous creeks, I also rode a lot of the Brockway country southwest of Circle.

In the early 1980s, I saw a lot of the Little Belt Mountains through the ears of a horse and made many decisions related to moving, gathering, branding, and dealing with our own cattle. The Snowy Mountains to the east of the Little Belts was also an area where I packed salt and fencing materials to deal with cattle on a Forest Service permit in the mountains. Our young family relished the Swimming Woman Creek area, where they could play and pick berries and splash in the creek until I showed up with my horse. Then we would build a fire and have a barbecue.

One unforgettable day I rode out of the Snowy Mountain permit area on my birthday, September 18, in a blizzard. We were planning to gather in the mountain valley area and head the cows home. With the snow and wind raging, we just left the gate open. The cattle, who knew the route well, came down on their own during the blizzard. That early fall snow was typical of that country but in the long run just added to my horseback decision-making experience.

When our friends Dave and Judy Hedman took us to the U-L Bend on Fort Peck Lake, I got to see the mouth of the Musselshell River and realized that I had seen the full length of the Musselshell, most of it through the vantage point of riding a horse. That included the Harlowton and Martinsdale country. I always enjoyed the Musselshell, and I have ridden it on several horses including my Shane and Byron Berg's horses. One of them was a good mare named CJ who came from my old boss Warner Johnson, who was definitely a horse trader. The horses and I have seen the Musselshell from drought dry to flooding.

I have already mentioned my first experiences with the 29-section Ryan's Fork pasture on the Montgomery Ranch. Riding for them has included all of the country north of the Yellowstone River from Forsyth to Angela, northwest of Miles City. Dog Creek, Sunday Creek, Ryan's Fork, Rough Creek, Louis & Scotty Creek, Stellar Creek, and Rattlesnake Creek all have my pony tracks along or across them. South of the Yellowstone, I've ridden the Buttes, Eagle Creek, Rosebud Creek, and Cherry Creek. Working with Harstads, I saw parts of the Northern Cheyenne Reservation a-horseback.

So what decisions are made with that view through a horse's ears? Decisions include the best way to drive cows, the best way to enter corrals, getting through gates, getting after strays, holding the herd, which cows need culling, scattering riders, and finishing a job even if storms come up or other situations come up. I have learned mostly to be focused on that view ahead of me, sometimes considering what needs to be left until tomorrow if I'm working alone. The peaceful feeling of being one with the horse and yet being in control is one of the very best rewards for being a cowboy.

Some of that time a-horseback has, of course, been spent on horses other than my own. From the time I spent at the Canfield Place, I broke, rode, and mostly enjoyed getting to know and use a variety of horses. This experience is part of what I wanted to share in this book because the more horses I got to know the more I understood how they think and work and what I'm looking for in a good horse and sometimes a great horse.

BOOMER

When I went to work on the Montgomery Ranch, I was assigned Boomer, who had been about half broken by other hands. I kind of hated to start riding him because he had never been taught to be bridle-wise. A rider would pull on the reins, and he would just throw his nose in the air. He was a big, powerful horse, and his attitude bordered on dangerous. I just kept working with him, teaching him to flex. I used a wire twist O-ring snaffle bit with a pretty good bite for more control. I would hold the reins, and when he would give the least little bit, I would release him. He finally got it figured out.

After about a year, I put Boomer in a leverage snaffle bit. He could be running full out, and when I pulled back just a little bit, he would start shutting down. Boomer was really good at heeling calves. The only real complaint I had was that he was dangerous when I tried to trim his hind feet. He would kick and rebel because he had been started wrong and hadn't learned to handle anything related to his feet.

One of the best stories on Boomer was when Montgomerys were trailing the big steers up north one spring. A number of the steers had foot rot and big swollen feet. Jim Chandler on Sparky and I on Boomer decided to doctor them, and we roped and doctored 12 in one day. We were riding home and came across a steer with a loop of barbed wire around his neck, dragging about 20 feet of wire behind him. Jim said, "Well, I'll kind of wait here. You see if you can get a rope on him, and we'll take that wire off." Boomer never even looked at the wire, just put me right in position to get the steer roped. Jim heeled him. The two horses stretched the steer out, and I got the wire off the steer.

Eventually, Boomer was sold, and I was sorry to see him go. He was a great example of a horse that was started out wrong by a poor trainer but had the intelligence to learn with the right handling and training. Occasionally, a horse trainer will run into a horse that is never going to cooperate and learn, sometimes because of being too spoiled and sometimes because of disposition. However, that kind of horse is the exception. Most horses just require guidance and days and miles of use to get up to their potential. Both most horses and most cowboys get better at what they're doing if they have productive work and days to do it. The wonderful thing is being able to achieve that together with mutual respect.

EAGER BEAVER

I have said a fair amount about training young horses. However, sometimes horse training takes some more extreme methods. I was working with a three-year-old named Eager Beaver. This little black horse was in use during calving time, but he was defiant. His ears were back all the time, and his jaw was clenched. If you came to a gate and stepped off him, he would fly back. One day I rode up on a knoll and pointed him towards home, then turned and rode the other way. He made one jump to dive into bucking, and I caught him and held him up with the reins. I trotted him over some rough country, and the farther we went, the madder he got.

My wife had come up to the camp, and our neighbor Owen wanted help branding. The evening before, I showed Cherie the gates to open for me along the eight miles to the neighbor's camp. She opened the gates, and I galloped Eager Beaver the full eight miles to the camp. Owen wasn't there, so I trotted two miles up the fence and back. When I got back and Owen was there, we gathered the cattle. I tied Eager Beaver to the fence and didn't water him or anything. Owen decided he had better haul us home.

That whole experience humbled Eager Beaver, and from that point on, he was a good horse. He worked well, but he still loved excitement. Later we were trailing pairs to another pasture across a neighbor's land. I was in the back by myself and about 15 calves came running back. That's a challenging deal! They ran past us, and Eager Beaver and I built to them and got beside them, got them turned, jumped a washout, and got them back in the bunch. I stopped Eager Beaver then. He had his ears up and was just strutting, so proud of himself.

Eager Beaver was a horse who couldn't be bored. He'd have to make his own excitement by spooking at things or jumping sideways or whatever. If you galloped him up a hill, he would be fine for a little while until he got bored again. I quit using him for just riding for that reason. He turned out to be an excellent calf-heeling horse for branding. When I started out with him, he was a little spooky about things. I would let my dally slide and let the calf get farther back so Eager Beaver had to pull harder. About the fifth or sixth calf, he would be doing really well.

LLOYDIE AND BROWN SHORTS

Lloydie was a Sure Fine horse, grey with black feet, and a tall, slim horse who was pretty well built. He was a fun horse to ride when things got western. He loved to run and turn something hard and be really collected and cool about it. Lloydie would buck on occasion.

As he got older, Lloydie took pretty good care of himself until he was needed, and then he was all horse. One of the most fun occasions was when I was trying to corral a bunch of cows at the north end of Dog Creek in the eastern part of the ranch. It was always tough to get cows started through the gate there. Lloydie and I would get them close to the gate, hold them and then push on them a little. They would bust past the gate, and Lloydie would take after them full tilt and bring them back. We did that several times and finally got them through the gate.

Lloydie had a half-brother named Brown Shorts who would buck several hands off sometimes and one of them all the time. He got that name from a hand who said the horse would scare the shit out of you with his bucking. I never had much trouble with him. I would spin him a bit and kind of untrack him.

If a horse is tight and humped up and the rider goes straight, he's going to buck. However, if the rider spins him and gets him off the track of heading straight out and bucking, that can stop him. I can't emphasize enough the importance of reading horses, sensing what they are going to do, and learning the best techniques for dealing with the situation. If the rider is the one in charge, horses can learn to be their best selves. I came to the point of enjoying Brown Shorts, who had a good fast walk and could really run when I needed him.

ROCKET

Rocket was a stud Montgomerys got as a colt from a rancher near Hardin. He was an Azure-Te Leo-bred horse, which meant thoroughbred/quarter horse breeding for speed and Leo heavily muscled breeding for cow work. I rode him as a three-year-old and on for the following several years.

Rocket was a fun, smooth horse to ride. I'd get him in time for gathering bulls and use him for weaning and for spring branding. I roped off him as well as used him for general cow work. Most every day was a good day with him. He handled himself well in rough country and in slippery conditions. He was willing and capable.

The first crop of colts out of him included six good stud colts that I halter broke through the winter. I got to tying them in the barn and giving them their oats. One day I left the door open in the morning. When I came back, they were all standing in their stalls waiting for their oats! All of the colts were sold. A year or two later the ranch kept a couple of yearlings that turned out to be good saddle horses.

Rocket was both a reliable saddle horse and a reliable stud. You could turn him in with geldings, and there would be no problem, which is not always the case with studs. Then came the day when he broke a hind leg and had to be put down. I sure missed him.

THE STUD

I always just called him "The Stud." He was a buckskin horse Montgomerys bought at age five from my friend and neighbor rancher Jack Lund. He was a smaller quarter-horse-type horse with extremely good legs and feet. He was bred by Larry Grantier from Winnett, a horse breeder I liked. I have already mentioned Hank, a quality buckskin from Grantier's string. The Stud was a really sensible young horse to ride. He was a horse you could bust out as hard as you could go to turn something, but when you had it done and stopped him, he would just drop his head and cooly walk off.

I used The Stud a lot for gathering bulls, fall weaning, and spring branding. He was okay around geldings like Rocket. One year our neighbors the Schiffers were trailing down. One woman and I were in front holding the cows back. She was riding a mare I hadn't noticed, and The Stud was just fine with it. His only fault was he had a bad mouth and had to have his teeth floated twice a year.

76

Unfortunately, that is something he would pass on to colts. I wound up with one of those colts, my good horse Comet whose teeth problems I've already mentioned.

The first calf I roped off The Stud had gone through the fence. I roped the calf, but the calf went to bucking and bellering and scared The Stud. I had a heck of a time getting things settled down but managed to get the calf choked down next to the fence and shoved through. After that, when I took a rope down, The Stud would be scared, but he finally got over it.

A year or two later I roped a bum calf in heavy gumbo and got him tied down. When I went to get back on The Stud, my boots were so caked with gumbo that I couldn't get them into the stirrups. I finally got the mud off one boot and got it into the stirrup, but the other leg was so heavy I just about couldn't swing it over the horse. I finally got the mud pulled off. During all of that, The Stud just stood there just fine.

When The Stud was older, one spring the boss said, "Well, we're going to brand a bunch of calves at the corral," a corral right next to the mare pasture. I unloaded The Stud and got on him. Then I told the boss, "Well, if you see me headed to the mare pasture, just gather me up next fall." He really got a kick out of that.

DILL WEED

One midwinter with deep snow, we were gathering some cattle at the Draper Place north of the Montgomery home place on the Yellowstone. Boomer had been used a lot, so I asked Kent's grandson Keeley Montgomery if I could borrow Dill Weed. Dill Weed had been bucking regularly and really being a problem. I got on and right away he went to bucking and spinning. His rear end slipped out from underneath him and stopped that. Then I galloped him for a couple of miles and had foam running off him. From that point on, he was a completely different horse. He worked well for others. After he was sold to a rodeo producer, he was used both as a ranch horse and as a bucking horse.

In the course of my time working on ranches, I met a number of unforgettable horses. Van Blankenship bought a horse named Gypsy who was really a good horse, probably one of my favorites. He had a burst of speed that would just about break your back. He was stout and powerful, a good roping horse.

CHAPTER 23

GOOD HANDS

It's about impossible to talk about horses and cowboying experiences without talking about hands. From the time I started working for George Canfield, who was that rare combination of an excellent boss and an excellent hand, I have been aware of developing as a hand myself and observing what kinds of other hands I was working with.

What do I mean by "hands"? Hands are men and women working for ranches, often called ranch hands, and in general, they are expected to do all kinds of ranch work. In more modern times, it's possible to be a hand and never get on a horse, using four-wheelers and pickups instead. But in the days when I started in this business, being a hand required being on a horse, and there were many people who did it all right and some who did it very well. I've already mentioned Tiny Ottun, who was an outstanding hand, not only for ranch work but also along with his wife Lynda and their daughters was a barrel racer and futurity winner.

When I quit winter feeding and went to spring, summer, and fall work only on the Montgomery Ranch, they hired a very capable hand named Shorty because he's so tall. Shorty and I have done a lot of jobs together, and I respect him for his work ethic and capability a-horseback. His wife Rachel also joins us for some riding and for brandings, and their son Jake does his part, choosing to be on a four-wheeler.

During the first year on Montgomerys' crew, I wound up calving heifers. Charlie Pierson, an old feller who had been a good hand all his life but on the extremely reckless side, was one of those colorful people everyone had a story about. Charlie was helping me put the pairs out of the calving pasture. One time we had five pairs and got to the out gate. I got the gate open and got back with Charlie, and we went to push them through. The calves just blew by us running back. I said to Charlie, "I wonder what Kent would say about that?!" And he said, "Don't worry about that kid; I keep him in line!" This was a man in his 80s talking about my boss, who was in his 70s. I've chuckled about that ever since.

The funniest story Charlie told about himself involved him and another old hand, Duffy Hafer. They were camped with a trailer north of the Yellowstone and had some steers to trail home. They got up one morning to pea-soup fog and deliberated about the best thing to do. They finally saddled up and took off herding the steers, turning by instinct and following trails as best they could. They went for hours. When the fog cleared, there Charlie and Duffy were, practically right back to the camp! Needless to say, they had to start over.

Charlie's Corner was a corner near Montgomerys' feed lot where Charlie had a house for a while. We branded there a lot, and I could tell a lot of stories. North of the corner is one gap through the badlands. I was riding my big roan Tom, and we were gathering mares and colts out of that pasture in preparation for branding the colts. We were chasing the bunch when the mares took off and went through the gap and around the end of a ridge, headed up the coulee. I met them and got them turned back to where they were supposed to go. That was one of the times I was really glad I had a good horse like Tom under me.

Other good hands included the Newmans – Albert and his sons Wally and Howard – who were special neighbors and also ran my cows for a few years. They owned the Rolston camp north of the Radeen camp where I lived, and we had some exciting times there chasing and corralling yearlings. Eventually, the Rolston camp became part of the Montgomery Ranch, and along with the deal acquired another colorful friend and good hand, Owen Badgett. Owen had been willing to help us as neighbors with things like gathering yearlings and weaning calves.

Owen liked to be the boss, but he was a capable hand and good to work with when we were in a tough spot. He had worked for the BLM in the Southwest when they were gathering mustangs out of the desert, so he knew how to run horses as well as cattle. Owen was also a teamster who enjoyed using a team and wagon to feed.

Owen was one of several hands I've worked with through the years who were born 100 years too late. These were men who would have been at home teamstering a chuck wagon or herding cattle up from Texas, sleeping with a bedroll and living on simple grub. I shared with them the enjoyment of just being out in the great outdoors, trailing along on good horses. Another good hand who would fit in that category is Morris Ware. Morris has cowboyed his whole life, enjoys driving teams and anything a-horseback, and also being a pick-up man, which takes real horse skills. He is at home in the Ingomar country.

One of the hands I had a lot of fun working with on the Montgomery Ranch was Jim Chandler. I appreciated the fact that once we set a plan, he'd stick with it. We did a lot of cowboying. Things worked smoothly between me and Jim, and I can't remember any wrecks. One of his favorite sayings was, "We were in over our heads and didn't even know it." There were times that was very true.

We were gathering longhorn bulls out of the Van Burton pasture at Dog Creek. We had them all gathered and were started down. One yearling bull jumped the fence and got back with the heifers. Jim just roped him and said, "Go get the trailer." We loaded the yearling in the trailer. We didn't have any more trouble that day. That's a good example of how things worked with us. He's also the hand I was working with when we dealt with that yearling trailing all the wire.

Jim was a great cook; he made some of the best beans and stew I ever had. His specialty was roast beef, and his method was to start the roast and potatoes in the oven on really high heat for 15 minutes, then turn the heat way down to slow cook all day. We could always come home to a great meal after a long day. I always appreciated that about Jim; whether it was my camp or his camp over at Dog Creek, he had supper figured out.

One day he set a roast and we took off east to the big pastures I've mentioned. We did a lot of cowboying that day. At almost sundown, we rode back to the horse trailer. As we loaded up the horses, Jim said, "Do you suppose I turned down that roast?" We headed back to the Dog Creek camp, and I went to unload the horses and turn them into the pasture while Jim headed for the house. He opened the door, and smoke came billowing out! I finished up, and when I walked in the door, I asked, "Is it done, yet?" "Smart ass!" The potatoes were nothing but burnt shells. The very center of the roast was barely edible. So, we ate, and we laughed about that meal for years.

Other good hands around my age have included Kent and Kirk Montgomery, both of whom were often along when we were trailing cattle from the home place by the Yellowstone River up to one or another of the ranch camps, or trailing them back home. Another Montgomery hand for several years was Bob Corbin, who always willingly helped me out when I needed it. He was always good help, a very capable hand a-horseback.

Another guy I first ran into when we moved to Rosebud was Ken Simmons. Both of us were kind of down and out, and we helped each other a lot and rented pasture together. I helped him start breaking a team of saddle horses to pull his hay wagon. Ken and I helped ranchers like Art Polich gather yearlings and for brandings We also did some team roping at his place; he got some roping steers and I enjoyed the practice roping using Pretty Boy and Tom. When I had cattle on Van Blankenship's place in the late 80s, a neighbor rancher was Hugh Espy. I rode with Hugh and helped Hugh and his wife Holly with branding and later weaning calves.

Not all the good hands around are older guys like me. Every time I see a Ranch Rodeo with primarily young hands showing off their horseback skills, roping, etc., I feel like there will always be young men and women who believe in quality cowboying and horsemanship. I personally have really enjoyed riding with some younger hands, including my three kids, all of whom qualify as great hands. I've mentioned Denver Woods and the time in the snowstorm when I said, "Why would anyone want to retire when we're having this much fun?" Besides Denver, some other fine young hands have shared days or months with me.

Back in the Little Belt Mountains days, an outstanding young rider named Greg Berg joined me for a massive job of treating foot rot, a very contagious disease that lames up cattle by affecting the soft tissue between the "toes" of the foot. Antifungal powder and antibiotics are used to treat the cattle, which must be roped one at a time.

Also, that summer, Greg and his brother Steve helped us out on a challenging branding day in those mountains. We set up panels for a portable corral. The young men and I separated the calves into the corral and prepared for branding. While our small children, including the baby in a basket, hung around outside the corral, Cherie branded and vaccinated while the Berg boys wrestled the cattle. I did most of the roping and the castrating and any dehorning. It was a big day, but we got it done and I always appreciated the willingness and capability of the Berg brothers.

At my present job, I've enjoyed times with Logan Eayrs, Jake Gilman, Bev Knuths, Teresa Certalic, and other fine young riders. I have to comment that some of these young people were in the saddle at an early age and others learned while I knew them. The years of experience help, of course, but the years are not nearly as important as the interest and persistence. All of them made days of gathering cattle, branding, and other work fun instead of just labor. And I've thoroughly enjoyed brandings that included my son Clint and his five boys, all of whom can ride horses and wrestle calves tirelessly. Grandson Jordan has taken the most interest in riding and roping and helps heel calves at branding time.

CHAPTER 24

PARTING THOUGHTS

One of my wife's favorite stories starts with the fact that in these years I am home for the winter because I no longer feed cattle for the Montgomery Ranch. By early to mid-March, I return to my five-and-a-half-day job at the Radeen Place ranch camp. I am so used to being productive that sitting idle in the winter isn't me. I find projects around our place, and my saddles and tack get well cleaned and oiled every winter. However, by late February I run out of both projects and patience and get restless and a bit crabby over needing something to do.

Meanwhile, my big horse Tucker is exactly the same way. He isn't mischievous the way Hank was, but he gets impatient and irritable, pacing and obviously needing to go to work. Cherie loves to watch the morning that I load my duffle, goods, and tack into the pickup and hook onto the horse trailer, ready to head north. Tucker loads immediately, and he has a spring in his step that matches my own. We both act 10 years younger, headed back to work and the heady freedom that goes with it.

None of us know how long we'll live or how long we'll be fit to do what we love. I can just say that my life will be good as long as there are horses in it. I deal with some lower back trouble and find it interesting that I can get stiff and sore driving the pickup or four-wheeler and even more so on the big, rough-riding road grader. But I don't get that way when I'm on horseback. My chiropractor explained that for people like me who have ridden for years, the motion of riding is actually therapeutic for the back.

In closing, Winston Churchill once said, "The outside of a horse is good for the inside of a man." I have to add that the inside of a horse is equally good for the inside of a man. Horses can be part of being a better person, of feeling peace and ease as well as success when the day goes well and the jobs are accomplished. I love going out to the barn and feeding them in the morning. At our place, feeding oats or cake requires haltering each one and feeding them in separate stalls so that the horse at the bottom of the pecking order gets his feed as much as the horse at the top. I also love unsaddling them and turning them out at the end of the day's work.

A fun thing I learned from one rancher was to watch a hard-used, sweaty horse cool and clean himself by rolling on the ground. We used to count the times he rolled over and multiply that by $100 to determine his "worth." I can honestly say that no matter how many times they roll, horses are worth their weight in gold for what they do for the inside of a man.

Are there more stories? You bet! And it's important to me to keep working, keep cowboying, and live for some more stories. I have a favorite set of pictures taken by a friend that shows a day we trailed yearlings home. When I look at them again and again, I like the looks of myself and other hands on good horses.

I also like the looks of the cattle trailing out, moving across the Eastern Montana prairie I've cherished all my life. Those pictures are their own story. Just give me that view through a horse's ears of the trail ahead, and I'll make decisions and be glad every time the day turns out right and the sunset sees me smiling.

SEASONING

I am blessed with a peaceful prairie day.
The old horse beneath me steps along,
Hooves meeting earth with years of knowing,
Confidently, like a familiar friend.

The breeze that has stroked these hills for centuries
Carries scents of grass curing in the sun,
Wildflowers flagrant in full bloom
And pines which have thrived each warm season
With sticky, strong-scented cones and needles.

Sage grows pungent in the afternoon heat.
Snows and rains have carried away bits
Of badlands above me, deepening creases,
Smoothing the hills rounder, gentler with time.

All nature grows older, ripens and renews.
I sip at life, like mellow, aged wine,
Savoring the full-bodied flavor that comes
Only with passing years and seasoning.

C.J. Heser

MEET THE AUTHORS

*Doug Heser was born and raised on a farm northeast of Vida, Montana. He graduated from Wolf Point High School and began raising his own cattle and working for ranches. He served in the U.S. Army from 1967-69, most of the time in Germany in the 4th Armored Division, Mortar  Batallion. He broke and trained horses and worked as a ranch hand for ranches throughout eastern and central Montana while continuing to have his own cattle. He and Cheryl met at Vida and were married in 1974, 50 years ago. He continues his career, working for the Montgomery Ranch primarily at a ranch camp north of Forsyth. Doug is a member of the Knights of Columbus and Montana Farm Bureau and enjoys being a father, grandfather, and great-grandfather, telling stories and visiting with anyone in the ranching industry.

*Cheryl Heser was born and raised in Billings, Montana. She graduated from Billings Senior High School and earned a Bachelor's Degree from Eastern Montana College and a Master's Degree from Lindenwood University. She taught English, Spanish, and Journalism until 1997 when she became Director of Rosebud County Library. At the state level, she won the Media Award for her radio show Library Connections and was the 2014 Sheila Cates Librarian of the Year. In October 2022 she was recognized in the U.S. Congressional Record as Montanan of the Month for excellence in education and performance of living history. Cheryl is the published author of "Walking at the Speed of Light: Following Jesus in Grief and Joy," based on the death of their youngest son. She shares music with the community, writes a column for the local newspaper, and loves family time.

Doug and Cheryl at The American Rodeo, Globe Field, Dallas, Texas, in 2023.

Doug and Cheryl on the four-wheeler at the Radeen Place ranch camp, Montgomery Ranch north of Forsyth.

www.ingramcontent.com/pod-product-compliance
Lightning Source LLC
Chambersburg PA
CBHW041628140626
46547CB00031B/1560